CLIO CONFUSED

Recent Titles in
Contributions in American History

The American Grocery Store: The Business Evolution of an Architectural Space
James M. Mayo

Reexamining the Eisenhower Presidency
Shirley Anne Warshaw, editor

From Nationalism to Secessionism: The Changing Fiction of William Gilmore Simms
Charles S. Watson

American Political Trials: Revised, Expanded Edition
Michal R. Belknap, editor

Southern Agriculture During the Civil War Era, 1860–1880
John Solomon Otto

"Worthy Partner": The Papers of Martha Washington
Joseph E. Fields, compiler

The Moment of Decision: Biographical Essays on American Character and Regional
Identity
Randall Miller and John R. McKivigan

Christian Science in the Age of Mary Baker Eddy
Stuart E. Knee

Northern Labor and Antislavery: A Documentary History
Philip S. Foner and Herbert Shapiro, editors

Loyalists and Community in North America
Robert M. Calhoon, Timothy M. Barnes, and George A. Rawlyk, editors

Abraham Lincoln: Sources and Style of Leadership
Frank J. Williams, William D. Pederson, and Vincent J. Marsala, editors

Zebulon Butler: Hero of the Revolutionary Frontier
James R. Williamson and Linda A. Fossler

CLIO CONFUSED

Troubling Aspects of Historical Study from the Perspective of U.S. History

DAVID J. RUSSO

Contributions in American History, Number 163
Jon L. Wakelyn, Series Editor

GREENWOOD PRESS
Westport, Connecticut • London

Library of Congress Cataloging-in-Publication Data

Russo, David J.
    Clio confused : troubling aspects of historical study from the
perspective of U.S. history / David J. Russo.
        p.   cm.—(Contributions in American history, ISSN 0084–9219
; no. 163)
    Includes bibliographical references and index.
    ISBN 0–313–29682–0 (alk. paper)
    1. United States—Historiography.   2. Local history.   3. United
States—History—Study and teaching (Higher).   I. Title.
II. Series: Contributions in American history ; no. 163.
E175.R868   1995
973'.072—dc20   95–7909

British Library Cataloguing in Publication Data is available.

Library of Congress Catalog Card Number: 95–7909
ISBN: 0–313–29682–0
ISSN: 0084–9219

First published in 1995

Greenwood Press, 88 Post Road West, Westport, CT 06881
An imprint of Greenwood Publishing Group, Inc.

Printed in the United States of America

The paper used in this book complies with the
Permanent Paper Standard issued by the National
Information Standards Organization (Z39.48–1984).

10 9 8 7 6 5 4 3 2 1

For Paul S. Fritz

Contents

Preface

This book is a series of closely related essays on particular facets of academic historical study. The book's parts were written, sporadically, over a period of several years after I became troubled with first one and then another aspect of historical inquiry connected to the work of historians of the United States. As I wrote on, it became clear that what I had to say could be organized into interconnected and sequential parts.

These essays are unusually personal in the sense that they are the product of much reflection on my part and were written without my soliciting a great deal of input or advice from academic colleagues and friends. In the broadest sense, what I say here derives from over thirty years of teaching a university survey course in U.S. history and from over fifteen years of teaching a specialized course on the Town in U.S. History. In both, I have always tried to present an integrated interpretation of the subject and have long favored emphasizing the nature of historical study as exemplified in the work of the historians I've examined.

My interest in synthesis and in historical interpretation dates back to the early 1970s, when I produced *Families and Communities: A New View of American History*, and continued through the 1980s, when my *Keepers of Our Past: Local Historical Writing in the United States, 1820s-1930s* appeared. Throughout these years, I have conscientiously read reviews of new studies relating to the entire field of U.S. history that have appeared in such journals as the *American Historical Review* and the *Journal of American History*. I have done so very self-consciously, with the avowed purpose of keeping abreast of overall scholarly developments in this most written about of all the historical fields of study.

"Part One: Common Confusions From A Historical Perspective" reflects what I've observed in contemporary society. Another historian would probably be struck by other confusions and would make other suggestions in the light of his or her historical perspective. "Part Two: Historians And Nations" involves a lot of my own reflection on my "field" of study, but, in addition, specifically for the essay, I have read a good deal of the best work on the nature of nationalism. "Part Three: Historians And Local Communities" draws not only on my years of teaching and synthesizing the scholarship relating to the history of towns in the United States, but also on a great deal of research that I've recently done for a projected history of towns in the United States.

"Part Four: Historians And Generalizations" is the product of my reflections on the importance and dangers of historical synthesizing.   Chapter 9 is openly prescriptive, a kind of guide or manual, and not an exploration of the strengths and weaknesses of the relevant historical scholarship. The list of historical questions in that chapter is wholly my own, built up over my many years as a historian with an ongoing curiosity about developments in academic disciplines related to history. "Part Five: Historians And Communication" stems from strongly held personal concerns about the state of the historians' craft. I've read studies on the history of writing specifically for Chapter 11. The lists of "verbal tones" and the "characteristics of human life" that appear in Chapter 11 are, however, wholly my own, constructed over a number of years.

I would like to thank Sarah Fick and Doreen Dixon of McMaster University's Humanities Word Processing Centre for their excellent preparation of the camera-ready copy of this book.

CLIO CONFUSED

Introduction

I consider this work the final volume in a trilogy of studies that began with *Families and Communities: A New View of American History* (1974) and continued with *Keepers of Our Past: Local Historical Writing in the United States, 1820s-1930s* (1988). These three volumes contain the results of many years of reflection on historical study from the vantage point of one who was trained to teach and write about the past within the "field" of American history.

As these chapters reveal, I now find such "fields" of study to be an artificial and inadequate means of dividing the human past for purposes of historical inquiry. But this is a recent insight for me, and the fact that I have spent many years of research on subjects as they relate specifically to the United States means that the questions I pose in the account that follows are raised from the perspective of the United States, the only area of the globe that I, as a "practicing" historian, feel knowledgeable about. If the views I express in this book gain any currency among academic historians, it will remain for future generations—trained differently and hopefully unconfined to politically defined fields—to communicate about the past in ways that I can now only imagine.

As my title suggests, I am quite troubled about many facets of the way academic historians, particularly those who deal with the United States, have been practising their craft. I am also perplexed by a number of what I call common confusions that the general public seems unnecessarily imprisoned by. I have felt compelled to bring to these confusions the insight and understanding available to me as a professional historian. Throughout this book, in some parts more obviously than in others, I have adopted both a critical and an exhortatory tone. I preach, warn, urge, scold, and plead. This is deliberate, for I am not only trying to understand what has reduced the effectiveness that academic historians should have in their society, but I am also attempting to persuade those historians that I know of ways for them to become more effective in what they do. But I am also chastened by the fact—as I indicate in Chapter 10, "False Generalizations in Historical Writing"—that my own assertions in these essays necessarily vault beyond the evidence I muster in support of them.

I believe that it is vitally important for both academic scholars and the lay public to get a better understanding and appreciation of each other's interests in our common, human past. One of the most profound intellectual problems that confronts modern society is the disjunction between what its intellectual elites comprehend and what the general population grasps. In the pages that follow, I have tried to demonstrate that neither group has—or should have—a monopoly over ways to find meaning in the past. I have attempted to demonstrate how the academic and the popular modes of thinking can complement and supplement each other, and how they can both contribute to that most human of mental undertakings: to understand the nature of life itself.

In this account, my inquiry, in effect, focuses on two contrasting perspectives: the individual's and humanity's. I contend that all historical study confronts two irreducible entities: the individual human being and the human species. Humans divide themselves into various groups, but each human being belongs to a varied, individualized array of groupings, and it is, therefore, from the individual's perspective that historians most insightfully study the past.

Human groups themselves are not distinctive entities in the same way that individuals are. Such groups have not been unique in the way they live, even though they have typically claimed they have been. Thus, for purposes of historical study any human group is an incomplete entity: identifiable in some ways, indistinguishable from others in other ways, and divided among themselves in still other ways. Only the individual human being has a uniqueness that allows the historian/biographer to demarcate a subject whose space or territory remains constant throughout his or her treatment of it.

If historians continue to study human beings collectively, in society, then the only perspective that is as constant and unchanging as that of the individual human being's is that of humanity itself, not the groups it has divided into. The most fruitful way to study the human past collectively is from a global perspective—that is, to select a particular subject and to examine it as it has existed all over the world. Only then can one gain a sense of proper proportion, of varied patterns and territorial configurations, of overall change and stability through time. If historians continue to study groups, then they should become far more aware than they have been of movable contexts or vectors, of differing shapes for different facets of their group's history—in size, sometimes greater than the group, sometimes smaller than the group, but rarely exactly the same as the group.

In focusing on these two perspectives—the individual's and humanity's, I have examined two themes in various ways throughout these chapters. The two themes are (1) the various groups that each individual human being belongs to—political, occupational, class, age, gender, sexual, religious, ethnic, racial—all of which can be made a basis for historical study, and (2) the protean shape of any human group or "community," depending on the aspect of its life being examined. My repeated references to these themes have, once again, been deliberate, for my purpose has been to demonstrate their centrality to many aspects of historical study as practiced by academic historians. Therefore, I believe this is justifiable repetition, a conscious device whose value is that with each new reference the themes become clearer.

In Part One, I examine several popular forms of intellectual befuddlement and try to show how our collective understanding of the aspects of life so involved benefits from the application of a historian's vantage point. People identify with various human groupings, and it is a mistake to think that their political communities are the only ones worthy of serious attention. People hold inconsistent views about the relationship of the government and the economy, religion, liberty and equality, and democracy and elitism, and I try to point out those confusions. It is common to think that human-made traditions are unchangeable rules, and I attempt to give examples taken from various facets of life.

In Part Two, I examine what seems to me to be the true nature of nations and why they are inadequate as a basis for fields of historical study. In Part Three, I focus on local communities in an effort to define them, providing definitions of such communities as offered by amateur historians, social scientists, and myself. In fact, both parts two and three deal with the concept of community, which historians have found to be most central to the ways they have organized the human past into fields of study. I conclude with the assertion that community has come to have a much broader definition, embracing all the groups that human beings have historically identified with, and not just "place" communities such as empires and nations and towns and cities.

In Part Four, I try to show that there are more effective ways for academic synthesizers to present general accounts of historical subjects than has been the case thus far. But I also caution all academic historians—synthesizers and specialists alike—against claiming too much, from reaching conclusions based on partial research, and from turning individual, identifiable human beings into faceless abstractions through the presentation of statistical evidence.

In Part Five, I attempt to show that, as long as scholars present their findings in the form of verbal communication, academic historical writing would immeasurably benefit from a conscious effort to emulate the best "writers," those whose writings have become classics. This could be done by writing in varied verbal "tones" (not just the objective tone) and by focusing on the basic characteristics of human life (not just on why human life has evolved into what it is now, important as that is).

I

COMMON CONFUSIONS
FROM A HISTORICAL
PERSPECTIVE

1

Identities

What is the United States? It is a nation. Who are Americans? They are the citizens of the United States. The United States and Americans are, therefore, political entities—nothing more and nothing less. I believe we would all understand contemporary life with much greater clarity if we remembered this deceptively simple fact.

It is important for us to realize that nations and their citizens are specifically political creations that fall far short of defining us as individuals, that they are only one form that human identification takes, a form more limited in its effects on us than we usually recognize. Human beings exhibit many forms of identity—age, gender, sexuality, occupation, class, ethnicity and race, language, and (religious) beliefs—and our political identity is one of these. Ethnicity and race, religious beliefs, and language have historically shared with political affiliation the capacity to provoke people into forming durable human groups that are deeply important to their members. (By contrast, age, sexuality, gender, occupation, and class have not yet exhibited this capacity.)

Nations cover the globe; virtually everyone on earth is a citizen of one of them. Nations have in various ways become sovereign; that is, they have assumed ultimate political authority over those who inhabit their territory. Our political affiliations—national, state, municipal—are obviously important. Governments regulate or affect virtually every aspect of our lives. In the world at large, such groups as diplomats, armed forces serving abroad, and athletes on national teams represent "us": upholding national interests, competing, sometimes fighting or even dying for our nation. But although governments in the modern world have come to exercise great authority over human life, they have never developed the capacity to influence their citizens to such an extent that the nonpolitical aspects of their lives have become "nationalized," compartmentalized, made distinctive or unique.

It is nationalism—that cluster of myths and symbols and memories and sentiments that bind us to our nation—which has created a disposition in citizens of particular nations to believe that all the dimensions of their lives—and not just the political one—are somehow different. The problem with nationalism is that it divides human beings in distorted and artificial ways, creating a sense of group solidarity beyond that which actually exists. Nationalism falsely extends political distinctions into other categories of human activity and behavior.

Americans are predisposed to think that there should be American art and entertainment, American sports, American science, an American economy, an American religion, an American philosophy, an American society, an American character—all national in scope, all particularly American. The question I want to pose is why should a group of people who have organized themselves into a unique political entity actually be different from other people in the other dimensions of their lives as well? My answer is that nationalism induces citizens to seek and then to think they have found national characteristics in all aspects of their existence.

But it is clear that there is no necessary connection between a people's political identity and the other aspects of their lives. If you consider the world and its inhabitants cartographically, the global "boundaries" for each aspect of human life clearly differ from all others. For example, political territories rarely coincide with linguistic, religious, ethnic, racial, or geographic territories. Furthermore, in what possible sense does a particular style or content of art or of thought embody a whole nation? What traits of character can truly represent a particular nation's entire citizenry? In what meaningful way can economic activity "belong to" a nation? There has never been a nation in all of human history whose citizens have been different in every aspect of their lives from all the other politically defined groups around them. The fact is that the economic, social, cultural, and intellectual dimensions of life have an autonomy of their own. Their natural shape or boundaries rarely coincide with political territories of any kind.

It isn't possible to define a specifically American national character, in spite of the efforts of a host of commentators and observers and scholars to do so. What traits apply to the entire population, to children, to women, to recent immigrants from the Caribbean, South America, Asia, or Europe, to Native Americans? Does being an American automatically mean you are boastful, loud, pushy, parochial? Does being an American mean that you behave in a certain way, clearly different from the way citizens of other nations conduct themselves? Those who advocate that a national character exists—in the United States or in other nations—have simply presumed that it exists and have not convincingly demonstrated how anyone can apply the notion of character to an entire politically defined group.

Similarly, it is not possible to define a distinctively American culture, in spite of the cultural nationalists efforts to find one. The music Americans compose, perform, and listen to is appreciated by people from all over the Western world and beyond. Styles that originated within the United States—jazz and rock—have come to be shared by others in various parts of the globe. Novelists, story writers, and playwrights all write about places and people and situations recognizably American—though, more accurately, reflective of a host of different settings both local and regional in scope. But the way these authors write—their style and technique—is shared with fellow authors across much of the globe. Choreographers in the United States come out of a much broader cultural tradition, both artistically and territorially. Architects in the United States draw on styles developed both here (in the case of skyscrapers and ranch-style houses) and elsewhere. Painters and sculptors in the United States exhibit enormous regional and even local variety as well as a sharing of styles and techniques common to much of the Western world.

What we are dealing with here is *culture in the United States*, not American culture—artistic activities that exist in great abundance in differing shapes and sizes that can be intensely local or regional or Western or even global, but that rarely coincide with political boundaries of any kind. Once again: observers, commentators, and scholars of "American culture," who exhibit a tendency to overgeneralize, have presumed, but have not demonstrated, that there exist cultural activities that somehow embody the artistic sensibilities of the entire national citizenry.

It is the same with other aspects of American life. There is, of course, no American language. Other means of communicating—audio and visual signs or gestures, musical notes, numbers, line and color, sculpted shapes—are either global in their dimensions or are shared by people in many parts of the world. Is there an American science? To ask this question is to presume that somehow science as practiced in the United States is different from the way it is practiced elsewhere. Is there an American religion and philosophy? What sense is there in regarding religious groups in the United States, almost all of which have originated elsewhere, as somehow distinctive? Is there any more sense in searching for an American philosophy, when Americans clearly rely on an amalgam of philosophical traditions developed in other parts of the world or, in the case of pragmatism, originating in the United States but taken up elsewhere?

Are there American sports? What games have originated in the United States and are only played here? Do not Americans share a sports culture that embraces much of the world? The fact that sports teams "represent" and compete on behalf of the inhabitants of towns, cities, and states, as well as the nation itself is a further indication that politically defined groups will use any feasible means to foster the growth of community identity and loyalty and spirit, even the competition of athletes, and is not evidence that American sports are somehow different in any basic way.

Is there an American economy, as journalists, commentators, analysts, government officials, and politicians constantly tell us there is? It is true that government in United States, at various levels, regulates, aids, and protects economic firms of various sizes and that the national government in particular provides a common currency and maintains trade regulations with the rest of the world. But what is distinctly American about the kind of economic activity that occurs within this nation's borders? Industrial capitalism in the United States fully exhibits the basic features of an economic system that now dominates the world's economy. Many firms within the United States are parts of larger economic units; others are local or at most regional entities. In any case, the actual size of economic enterprises does not coincide with the territories of political units of any kind. It is far more important that a firm be identified as an industrial corporation, say, and thus as an enterprise that shares essential characteristics with such firms all over the world, than it is to say that a firm is American.

Is there an American society? In one sense, there is: it can be said that a society is simply the nonpolitical life of the citizens of a particular nation. But, in my view, this is a very loose definition to give to this term. Americans lack a common ethnic or racial identity, but so do the citizens of other ethnically and racially varied nations, which means virtually all the other nations of the world. There have been "old-stock" Americans of British origins, but this element in the population has practically disappeared through intermarriage with others. The portion of newer immigrants from other parts of Europe as well as "Latin" America and Asia is quickly growing. And the native population continues to constitute a distinctive element within American territory. Americans share with the "Europeanized" parts of the world a particular form of class structure: a tiny upper class with enormous wealth and power, a large and varied middle class, and a relatively small lower class defined by its poverty. Notice that when someone refers to "our society," it is often unclear whether the reference is to the United States, North America, or the West more broadly.

Even with respect to government itself, the United States shares a presidential system with nations in other parts of the world and, in concert with other Westernized states, has developed welfare capitalism, with government support systems for education, health care, culture, the environment, and social security.

But, to repeat: the terms *United States* and *Americans* have a political definition. Americans would have a much clearer view of the world and of humanity if they realized that they are first and foremost human beings, each of whom has many forms of identity that he or she possesses concurrently and, hopefully, harmoniously. Each form of their identity embraces a different group of people with a different territorial shape. We would all be much better off if we developed an awareness of the fact that our national political identity is only one form of human identification, only one way that human beings divide and form groups. We should remember that, above all, we are human beings who share a common planet as well as common problems and opportunities. In the future, what we share will, I believe, come to be of greater significance than what has divided us.

2

Inconsistencies

In the Westernized or Europeanized parts of the world—those areas where Christianity, capitalism, democracy, and a social structure with a broad middle class have prevailed—there have been a number of fundamental inconsistencies in popularly held beliefs concerning government, the economy, religion, and society. These inconsistencies are so basic, so taken for granted, that they are rarely commented on, either by ordinary people or by intellectual elites, one of whose tasks is to observe and comment on such phenomena.

In one sense, this silence is amazing, because these inconsistencies are so obvious. In another sense, it is perhaps because they are so obvious that they need to be beyond discussion: Should people start to discuss them, perhaps the political, religious, economic, and social patterns of life which these inconsistencies silently support would unravel or rupture. But ordinary citizens in the Westernized world would benefit from public discussion of these inconsistent popular beliefs and attitudes, for it is my assumption that when people have a greater understanding of themselves and their world, the possibility for a better life for all is significantly enhanced.

*

One such inconsistency—one that involves both government and the economy—is the prevailing belief that there should be a privately owned and managed economy, but that government is to blame if the economy stalls or declines, even though the government does not own or even directly manage the economy. For its part, the government congratulates itself if the economy grows, even though it isn't primarily responsible for the growth.

Socialism, insofar as it has been associated with the public ownership of economic institutions or direct governmental management of economic activity, has never been popular in the West. Only where totalitarian communist parties have gained control of governments—in the former Soviet Union and (with the support of an imperialist, militarized Soviet state) in Eastern Europe—have governments "commanded" the economy in particular political jurisdictions. The citizens of these nations at least tolerated such an arrangement (between the late 1940s and circa 1990), for they did not get rid of such communist-led governments. Communism as a political phenomenon disintegrated from the top, not the bottom.

Elsewhere in the Europeanized portions of the globe, the vast majority of citizens—even where democratic socialist parties have formed governments—have not favored public ownership of the economy. Instead, there has been widespread support for (though always division over the pace and extent of) the development of "welfare-capitalist" states, that is, for the augmentation of governmental authority, so that the private economy is thoroughly regulated, and all citizens are provided with a minimum level of security and welfare. Westernized governments have also assumed significant fiscal and monetary and regulatory power to modify the natural, capitalistic economic cycle of growth and stagnation or decline.

Thus, in the late twentieth century, the government and the economy—the public and private realms of material life—are thoroughly mixed. Perhaps it is because in all of the capitalist-dominated areas of the globe the political and economic aspects of life are so intermingled and yet remain clearly separated entities that Western citizenries have become confused and have oversimplified the complexities of their economic/political system by adhering to fundamental inconsistencies in their attitudes toward the relationship between their governments and the economy.

If these citizens were to be educated in the true nature of that relationship, I believe that they could reorient themselves and say: O.K.!! Henceforth, we will not blame the government for every economic recession or depression. We will understand that, since the government does not own or manage the economy (and we don't want it to), then it cannot be blamed for what it does not control. We will insist that, through its monetary and fiscal policy and through its regulatory powers, it should do all it can to 'even out' the economic cycle, which is natural to a capitalist system. But we won't allow the government to take credit for economic growth, even though its policies may have contributed to that growth. We realize that political/economic relationships are complicated, that the political and economic aspects of our lives are profoundly intermixed, that we favor neither pure socialism (defined as government ownership and management of the economy) nor pure capitalism (defined as an economy largely unaffected by government). So, we won't expect our economic problems to be cured or solved by governments, nor do we expect a risk-free economic life, with guaranteed security and prosperity. This mixed system has risks in its operation and always will.

*

Another fundamental inconsistency in popular attitudes among those who live in Westernized parts of the world involves the widespread and growing belief it is not worthwhile to attend church services of or to become members of a religious body. For the first time in human history, significant numbers of people—at least in areas where Christianity is dominant—are living out their lives without any ongoing reference to religious belief. Such people have moved "beyond faith," either out of indifference or out of a sense that their material existence is all that is worth focusing on. (A much smaller, more intellectually oriented group has become agnostic, arguing that ultimate reality is unknowable and is by nature speculative.)

In a sense, Protestantism has triumphed in the West. Many Westerners, in a kind of "priesthood of all believers," state that their beliefs are private, being between themselves and God, and that they do not need or want to be involved in organized religion. In another sense, secular humanism has triumphed, both to the extent that the laws of the nations of the world have come to define the rules by which people live (thus giving a secular basis for the religious morality advocated by churches), and to the extent that such laws have become similar in the various political jurisdictions of the world, with "charters of human rights" contained in ever-larger numbers of national constitutional arrangements, as well as internationally, in the United Nations Charter.

And yet, perhaps it is because so many Westerners have a vague and amorphous relationship to religious belief and to churches that the vast majority, when pressed, still profess a belief in God and still mark the basic passages of life—birth, marriage, and death—with religious ceremonies. The fundamental inconsistency here is for one to move away from attendance and membership in a church at the same time that one still claims, at least in times of crisis, to believe in God and still allows life's transforming acts to receive a ceremonial religious sanction. In short, increasing numbers of Westerners are in a twilight zone where material life and spirituality coexist in a confusing and shadowy way. Such people are caught up in the inconsistency of denying the churches and religious belief a central place in their lives, at the same time that they are calling the churches out of hiding for ceremonial purposes, and at the same time that religious belief itself is generated only in times of crisis.

Such people fail to see that for faith to be vibrant and alive, it needs to be the metaphysical and ethical basis for life itself, and not something that people occasionally turn to in moments of crisis or during life's passages. If Christianity has lost its legitimacy as the professed faith of increasing numbers of Westerners, either literally or symbolically—as myth—then it is time for lapsed Christians to try to find a new faith—and a new myth—that better fits their sense of reality. I believe that secular humanism is the most compelling alternative faith for such Westerners. It offers the best chance for an understanding of reality that resonates with our current ways of knowing, and it is the best hope for the emergence of new myths, symbols, and liturgies based on humanity itself, and not, as in the past, on particular human groups.

Those caught up in this inconsistency should be able to say: Right on!! We shouldn't go on making light of religious faith at the same time that we continue to profess a severely thinned-out connection to it. We can't have it both ways! So, let's seriously try to reformulate our faith and find a new liturgy, myth, and symbol that connect with today's sense of reality. Let's search for the appropriate institutional expression (a new "church") for those who subscribe to our new formulation. And let's make our secular laws accurately reflect our ethical sense, if we are going to continue to allow, not God, but human judges and our peers (on juries) to deal with our infractions of those rules. In short, let's try to make faith, once again, the central expression of our sense of ultimate reality. Christianity is losing its long-term position as the embodiment of our civilization's collective faith. If we can't find a new faith, let's move boldly beyond faith and admit that the human propensity to hold beliefs on ultimate matters and to develop ethical codes are futile, indeed unnecessary, exercises. Let's truly live without faith, not partially, not out of indifference, not out of an unexamined sense that our material existence is all we have.

*

Another fundamental inconsistency involving popular attitudes is the widespread belief in political equality—equality under the law, equal human rights for everyone, equal voting and office-holding rights—at the same that there is a correspondingly widespread lack of belief in social and economic equality. People in the Westernized world assert their political equality while equally insisting on their social and economic inequality.

What makes this position seem coherent and sensible to those who hold it is their collective conviction that the right to hold property and wealth is a human right that all possess equally. In this sense, social and economic inequality are grounded in political equality. It is often said that all should have an "equal opportunity" to get rich. Ironically (and usually unnoticed), the right to accumulate wealth and property and the hoped-for equality of opportunity that is its political manifestation presume social and economic inequality, since people are so unequal in their origins and capacities and in the fortuitous circumstances that shape the material aspects of their lives.

Even the assertion that all must be politically equal is in reality much more a pious hope than a fact. Enormously unequal levels of political influence are exerted on politicians during campaigns and between elections. Lobbyists and organized special interests and large contributors to political parties have a far greater capacity to determine the actual composition of legislation and its application as law than do ordinary citizens, even though it is individual citizens who vote and determine the outcome of elections.

The fact is that most Westerners hold contradictory positions on the place of equality in their lives. Since the eighteenth century, there has been an evolving consensus in the West (except, from World War I to around 1990, in those areas whose people came under the domination of fascist or communist governments) that an ever-larger portion of the nation's population should be accorded political equality; should be allowed to be citizens and members in full standing of the polity or political community; and should be voters and officeholders and be granted protection of their civil liberties and their human rights, with equality under the law.

At the same time, there has been an equally firm consensus (except in those areas whose people tolerated communism) in support of the belief that people are, and ought to remain, vastly unequal in the social and economic aspects of their lives. Wealth has gradually replaced inherited status as the basis for a person's social position, and it has been as forceful a determinant as inherited status ever was. Among Westerners, wealth is equated with success. Wealthy elites are social models. The attainment of such wealth is the goal for most of the remainder of the population.

Nothing assures social peace and cohesion—and makes revolution for social/ economic purposes more unlikely—in the steeply economically/socially gradated Westernized populations than the fact that the rich are viewed as social models, not as oppressors to be violently obliterated. As long as there is a significant upwardly mobile element in the "middling" segments of these populations, violent change is unlikely. And nothing reveals the equation of wealth with success and poverty with failure more than the popular revulsion toward "welfare cheats." In stark contrast, only a mild rebuke is usually accorded the hugely more significant cheating carried on by business people who engage in white-collar crime. A poor person ("a failure") who acts unethically and illegally is subjected to far more popular censure than a rich person ("a success") who acts in a similar manner and on a much larger scale.

If Westerners face up to these contradictions in their position respecting the place of equality in their lives, they should then be able to say: All right!! Once again: We can't have it both ways. Either we grant equality the same place in the economic/social aspects of our lives that it plays in our political lives, or we should reconsider the validity of this vast network of equal political rights that we have worked out over the past two centuries. If people are naturally and perpetually unequal in their economic-social lives, perhaps they are equally and naturally unequal in their political lives as well. Perhaps the great Western experiment in the establishment of ever-broader political equality should be unraveled. Perhaps we should return to some version of the old "stake-in-society" argument that justified restrictive voting and officeholding and the protection of civil liberties to propertied adult white males! In any case, we have worked ourselves into a position based upon a giant inconsistency.

If, instead, we extend equality to the economic and social spheres, we need to think through how this should be done. What forms does the practical manifestation of equality—democracy: the theoretically equal participation of all in decisionmaking—take on in the economic and social spheres? Do we tax the rich to the point that the wealthiest are not enormously richer than the poorest? (In Western populations, the wealthiest 1 to 10 percent have often controlled as much as two-thirds to three-fourths of the of the wealth.) How do we gain popular approval of such a move if the rich remain social models: that is, remain the people that most others are trying to become? Do we offer a guaranteed annual income to the poor? If so, what would be the effect of such a move on the poor's attitude toward wealth accumulation, which has been at the heart of recent Western views of how society rightfully assumes its proper "shape"? Do we, through tax incentives, turn economic firms into cooperatives and thus entities owned collectively by all who work in them? If so, what happens to "outside" capital seeking investment outlets? Do we, through appropriate legislation, designate boards of directors as the ultimate decision-making body of all firms beyond a certain size, boards whose membership accurately reflects the composition of all who work in the firm? If so, how do we establish how many board members each type of a firm's workers are entitled to? What is the most "democratic" way to proceed in each of the above cases?

In short, to make our position on the place of equality in the political/economic/social aspects of our lives a consistent one will take a lot of frank, open, clear-headed discussion, argument, and action in ways not even yet imagined, simply because our inconsistent positions on these matters have not been sufficiently recognized, let alone become the basis for debate and change.

*

Another inconsistency stemming from popular attitudes is not confined to Westerners, but it is as a Westerner that I write about it. People everywhere perceive or assess others both as individuals and as members of various groups and, in the process, overlay what they perceive of an individual with group stereotypes and create contradictory and inconsistent assessments as a result. This is natural, for human beings have a dual capacity to particularize and to generalize. Life would be far too demanding and confusing for us to try to learn directly everything that is important to know about each individual we meet. So, we tend to categorize a person by the groups he or she is a member of, interacting in a kind of interpersonal "shorthand," responding on the basis of what that person's group affiliations tell us he or she is all about. But in our categorizations, we oversimplify or stereotype a person's behavior or personality in advance of knowing either in all its individuality.

Yet another duality that haunts our relationships with others is the dichotomy between our public friendliness with individuals and our private hostility toward the groups they belong to, or, in another formulation, our private hostility toward individuals and our public friendliness toward the groups they belong to. For example, it is common for people to say that "Some of my best friends are [Jews, Catholics, Protestants, and so on]," at the same time that these same people have privately held critical, stereotyped, oversimplified views of the very groups that their "best friends" belong to.

As a result of these dualities in the ways we perceive others, we can dislike individuals simply because of presumed personality or behavioral traits that we believe derive from their particular group identities. (I dislike John or Mary because he or she is Jewish, Catholic, Protestant, etc.) We can also dislike whole groups because of their presumed characteristics. (For example, note the enmities between the Serbs and the Croats or Bosnians; the Protestants and Catholics of

Northern Ireland; the Jews and Arabs of Israel/Palestine.)

We cannot expect to eliminate these ways of relating to others, for they are far too basic an aspect of human behavior. What we can do, however, is to modulate their most negative effects. We can become aware of how inconsistent and contradictory our views of others are, and how intricately related these restrictions are to the dualities of perception just outlined.

It should be possible to say: O.K.! I realize that what I think of John or Mary will always be an amalgam of what I perceive to be unique about him or her with an overlay of characteristics that I believe defines the various groups he or she is a member of. (Something is "so Protestant," "so Jewish," "so Catholic"; "so Italian," "so French," "so English"; "so like a woman," "so like a man"; "so like a young person," "so like an old person"; "so like a rich person," "so like a poor person.") It is important for me also to realize that John and Mary are unique individuals, however much their behavior is shaped by their membership in various groups, especially when they are with other members of their group (in the sense that group behavior influences and alters individual behavior). But I should be continuously aware that John and Mary are "live" individuals who go on through time and space, both in my purview and out of it, and exist in ever-changing circumstances and therefore can never be fully defined by me, either as individuals or as members of groups, which also evolve over time and space.

In other words, our capacity to know others is contingent and is quite limited. We can never "inhabit" their minds and bodies. We ourselves change over time and space and are ourselves members of groups that do likewise. Furthermore, those we consider members of our "own" groups, against which we measure other groups, are also unique individuals who are also members of groups we aren't members of, which greatly complicates the question of who is "ours" and who is "theirs". In short, let's try to understand that all individuals, whether considered separately or as members of groups, are all like us: beings of various identities based on gender, sexuality, age, occupation, class, ethnicity, language, belief—beings evolving through time and space, both alone and in groups and, like us, needing empathy and understanding.

*

The final popular inconsistency I'll examine involves the widespread belief that the purest forms of democracy are those that occur whenever limited, localized groups act on the basis of decisions made by all their members. I'm referring here to town meetings at which all voters decide on issues of concern to the local community (as in New England), as well as to corporate shareholders' gatherings, local labor unions, grass-roots protest or reform movements, neighborhood groups of all kinds, the local chapters of social or fraternal clubs, or any small-scale organization whose entire membership meets together in one place and time and makes decisions. The assumption here is that distant, representative bodies, such as provincial or national legislatures, or faraway elite groups of experts with superior technical knowledge, or the directors of large, sprawling organizations of all kinds are less democratic in their actions because they are less accountable to the wishes of ordinary individuals.

But those who believe that the purest forms of democracy involve the decisionmaking of local groups usually ignore the fact that such groups typically are also profoundly conservative. The conservatism I have in mind derives from a narrow, restricted sense of who "we" are and, by contrast, who "they" are—all those "others" who aren't members of the group. These presumably democratic localized groups tend to be highly suspicious of outsiders, to exhibit a vastly oversimplified view of hostile or indifferent foreigners, and, above all, to stress the purity and cohesion of the group itself, even though it divides at times on issues before making collective decisions.

Historically, the purest democracies have consisted of largely like-minded, small-scale groups that have been notably intolerant of outsiders. Until recently, these "democratic" groups have typically consisted of white, adult males within a hierarchically arranged "Western" civilization.[1] Pure democracy in this historically predominant version was restricted to particular groups of white men who organized themselves in such a way that there was equality of decision-making authority among themselves. But they did so in a civilization filled with hierarchical arrangements, a civilization that denied women and other races equality in many contexts. The inclusion of women and racial minorities has come about both as a result both of pressure from the excluded groups and of the conviction held by some of those already with authority that it is morally proper and politically and socially expedient for such reform to occur.

If democracy is also to include tolerance as part of its definition, if it is to make room for diversity, and it is to take account of varied forms of belief and behavior, then it is necessary to recognize the role of distant legislators and governors, of the experts and officers of large, varied organizations in bringing about varying degrees of social, economic, and legal equality for all the groups and individuals who comprise our contemporary Westernized society. For example, it was academics (particularly anthropologists and sociologists) who undermined racism as a respectable belief, not local groups of white people, some of whom have remained quite resistant to the notion of racial equality. Moreover (in the United States at least) it was national legislators representing varied, urbanized constituencies who, allied with protest groups, led the way for civil rights reform in the 1960s, not the representatives of the more homogeneous rural districts or states.

Other examples of this kind could be added, but the point would be the same: equality for minority groups and individuals has been achieved through the efforts of the minorities themselves and of sympathetic experts and technocrats and officials and legislators who have sometimes been decried as being the antithesis of democratically oriented local groups. Minority groups themselves have spawned protest or reform movements. But these movements have benefited from the allegiance of these "elites," who have thus played a role in creating of a broadened democracy, and in widening the ambit of liberty and equality.

By helping to add ever-more numerous elements in the populations of Westernized nations to the workings of democracy, such "elites" have perhaps unwittingly operated from a humanistic perspective. By breaking down the barriers between us and them, ours and theirs, insiders and outsiders, friends and strangers, by working to assure all individuals and groups various forms of liberty and equality, they have thereby reduced the significance of the multitude of particular human groups that exist in the world and have enhanced the importance of the world's one general group: humanity itself.

If democracy is to be linked to liberalism, in short, the very definition of democracy will have to be broadened to include at least two elements, elements that can be at odds with one another: that is, both the direct participation of all members of a group in decisionmaking and their acceptance or tolerance of others as having an equal right to form groups and to behave and believe in ways that contrast with "our" own.

If people, especially those active in local democratic groups, would only understand and appreciate this, to my mind, inherently dual character of democracy, then they could say: All right! Democracy isn't easy. In fact, I will undoubtedly feel the tensions that exist between what I now see as two fundamental aspects of it. I understand that it was as a result of efforts made both by minorities themselves and by the presumably "undemocratic" representatives and officers and experts of large and varied constituencies and organizations that minority groups and individuals have attained certain measures of liberty and equality, and not usually by efforts made by the purely "democratic" groups I've belonged to. Henceforth, I may want to act in concert with others who share my goals, but I should resist the temptation to join with only those who behave and believe just as I do. I should be accepting of people who may share my concerns, but at the same time are quite different from me in their occupation, class, race, sexuality, gender, age, religion or values or beliefs, and language. In other words, people of varied identities may want, for a variety of reasons, either to join or oppose a particular group that I am a member of. "Democracy" for me must involve tolerance and equality for all who wish to be members of "our" group or any opposing groups as much as it must involve decisionmaking by everyone in such groups.

*

The popular inconsistencies I have briefly explored in this chapter are deeply held and are not likely to be wholly given up by anyone reading these words. Human life abounds in inconsistencies and likely always will. But the forms these inconsistencies assume may change over time. It seems to me that one way to bring about what in my view would be highly desirable change is for people to be made aware of their more destructive inconsistencies. I hope this essay contributes to that end.

3

Traditions

Why is it virtually unimaginable that the clear result of an American presidential election would be contested? Why is it almost impossible to picture the Joint Chiefs of Staff taking over the government if displeased with the result? Why is it extremely unlikely that the losing candidate will try to take or keep office anyway? Instead, why are all those directly involved with the election's outcome so concerned to act according to the Constitution? The reason is that the politicians and military officers, as well as the voters, all believe in the constitutional system. They believe it has a legitimacy that places it beyond criticism as the basis for a functioning political order.

By contrast, why was President Gorbachev booed when viewing the Soviet Union's May Day celebrations in 1991? Can anyone imagine Stalin being booed, or Khrushchev or Brezhnev in a similar situation? Why wasn't Russian President Yeltsin captured by troops when he was perched on a tank in Red Square during the abortive coup during August 1991? Why were some of Gorbachev's final Presidential decrees simply ignored? What happened to centralized authority in the Soviet Union? What happened was that the communist government lost its legitimacy. An erstwhile authoritarian government lost much of its mystique, the aura of authority that had helped to sustain its autocratic power for three-quarters of a century.

By contrast, the student uprising of May 1989 brought China to the brink of cataclysmic political change. For a few days, observers from all over the globe could feel both the civilian population and the soldiers waiver between their accustomed allegiance to the communist government and a new openness to the student movement. The center of Chinese political authority was briefly shrouded with uncertainty. And then—the army crushed the dissidents and the communists reestablished their political authority. Why? The reason was that the army remained loyal to its own officers and those officers remained loyal to the government. In

China, the institutions that have autocratically governed since 1949 had not lost control: soldiers and civilians alike were unwilling to challenge the legitimacy of the communist government—and yet, they wavered.

Here are examples from three nations of the presence, the uncertainty, and the absence of political legitimacy.

Ordinary people rarely question the nature of their unexamined allegiance to a particular political system. Those systems with a high degree of legitimacy have attained their favored position only because those who live under them have been indoctrinated since childhood in the efficacy and desirability of such arrangements. People believe that these systems have an authority and "rightness" that, in reality, rests on tradition, on long-term, intergenerational durability, on the mystique, majesty, authority, and power that have come as a result of longevity and durability, and not from some superhuman source.

Rules and institutions and patterns of behavior do not retain their power because some superhuman police or military force coerces humans to obey. Who controls the police and the military? Why would the police and military enforce such rules and uphold the legitimacy of such institutions unless their members believed there was some compelling interest for them to do so? The lines of authority of any political system—whether democratic or autocratic, whether weak or centralized—hold only as long as there is a widespread belief in the legitimacy of that system.

In short, humans give allegiance to particular arrangements because they have taught each other to do so and because they have developed ways of reinforcing widespread allegiance: instruments of political coercion. If, for any reason, people fail to develop and sustain this kind of belief in the legitimacy of their rules and institutions, they can bring about   basic change in their political systems, although the timing and pace of that change have varied enormously.

It is important for ordinary people to understand that this is what characterizes their public life: that the rules and institutions by which they live are historically created and sustained and thus not immutable, unchangeable, all that can ever be. That which seems permanent, beyond question and debate, remains so because people believe it is so. People can invest their political systems with a majesty, aura, and mystery that sanctifies them and gives them an overwhelming legitimacy.

Of even more importance is the fact that this process of legitimizing political arrangements extends to all aspects of human life: to the economic, social, cultural, intellectual, religious, recreational dimensions, to all the settled, largely unquestioned traditions by which people live. There are no extraterrestrial beings forcing humans to live the way they do. There are no superhuman armed services coercing humans to comply with rules, and the behavior and activity that people have not already taught themselves ought to be obeyed or pursued.

Why don't those with little wealth rise up and take the property of the very rich? Throughout human history, in many kinds of economic and social systems, there has been a strong tendency for a small group of people to amass great wealth, while others have been able to accrue only modest or even paltry amounts. Why have social elites so rarely been the target of the remainder of the population? Why have those who in today's terms are millionaires or billionaires been able to live in relative safety in the same communities with those mired in poverty or those with far fewer material possessions?

The reason is that significant numbers of others want to become rich too. Social elites are models, not targets. Other people may envy them, but they also want to become like them. Through much of human history, social status—one's position in any given population—was determined by inherited rank or class. At the top of such hierarchical social structures were aristocracies, elites who had both wealth and power. As these aristocracies have declined around the world since the eighteenth century, the possession of wealth itself has become the chief determinant of social status. Hierarchical social structures that had been sustained by the inheritance of status have continued to exist because of the vastly unequal capacity of people to amass wealth.

The acquisition of wealth became a supreme value of those people around the world influenced by Europeans and their civilization. Wealth received a religious sanction through the Christian doctrine of the calling. According to this doctrine, all children of God had a God-given talent that it was their Christian duty to develop to its fullest extent. Wealth also received a political sanction. Property was a civil liberty: Everyone with full membership in civil society should have an equal right (or opportunity) to private wealth. That this equal political right produced social and economic inequality among those accorded it has received far less attention.

In all areas of the globe where a capitalistic form of economy prevails, the acquisition of wealth and the many benefits it bestows on its possessors has been a primary goal of most of the population. Industrialization has produced a large middling element—an element that used to consist of farmers and craftsmen—whose members seek to be upwardly mobile, to end life in a higher position (based largely on wealth) than the one in which they started. It is this aspiring middling element that assures the already-rich their security. A violent confiscation of the wealth of these elites is highly unlikely as long as there is a significant, aspiring, upwardly mobile middle class.

But people should realize that, even though the lives of our ancestors have always exhibited social and economic inequality, which has been one of the most deeply engrained of all human traditions, the reason the very rich can usually live in peace and harmony among the poor is that wealth itself has always been accorded such a mystique, an aura of power and authority, something of great value and desirability. If humans were to change their attitude toward wealth, diminishing its vast symbolic and real importance, the great gulf between the richest and the poorest would probably no longer be tolerated. Why? Because the middling element of the population would not be as focused on the goal of becoming rich too.

What might force this middling element to change its attitude toward the acquisition of wealth? One factor might be the imminence of environmental disaster. Another might be a capitalism that truly does produce a relatively few wealth-producing occupations alongside a lot of menial jobs with limited opportunity for the amassing of wealth. Either development—both of which are at least possible—would probably force the middle class to reassess its wealth-augmenting possibilities and to look again at the desirability of a few having so much, while so many have so little.

Since the 1940s, a growing majority of humanity has lived in urbanized communities, in large-scale human settings filled with strangers. Why don't those strangers assault us, rob us, kill us? Some do, but the number is very small compared to the total number of people moving about in these urban settings, going about their daily business. Why do we presume that most strangers won't accost us in some way?

The answer is: civility. As urban areas grew very rapidly during the nineteenth and twentieth centuries, a growing middle class developed a civic civility, a politeness, forms of peaceful, social interchange that allowed them as individuals to engage in work- or leisure-related activity in peaceful, harmonious ways. But, as historical traditions go, this one is of comparatively recent origin. Most human beings through most of human history have lived out their lives within the confines of rather small groups—in rural areas, in hamlets, villages, or towns. Urbanites who have recently moved to the cities from elsewhere often have difficulties adjusting to their new setting because it takes time to learn and to internalize the civility toward strangers that those born and bred in an urban setting have already mastered.

Indeed, the tradition of civic civility has encountered continuous difficulty over the past two centuries. The basic problem is that the tradition's appeal has been limited to the middle and upper classes. Those urbanites who live in relative material comfort are usually civil, but it is much more difficult for those who are in poverty to be so. The urban poor are much more apt to be rougher, more violent, less nice in their language and public behavior, and more likely to commit serious crimes against persons.

It seems likely that this tradition will continue to be classspecific as long as significant numbers of poor people are crowded into urban centers. Thus, the effort of the middle class, a class that grew to prominence as a result of industrialization and urbanization, to construct an urban society that functions peacefully and smoothly has thus far been only partially successful, and the tradition of urban civility has been one that only a part of society believes in.

Why do so many blacks in the United States live in urban slums, in poverty and ill-health and crime? Why don't the blacks work their way out of this setting? Why can't blacks be like other immigrants to the Western Hemisphere?

In order to understand the existence of black ghettoes, one has to confront a deeply engrained tradition of racism in the Europeanized portions of the globe. American blacks were enslaved and then segregated and all the while were perceived as racially inferior by the dominant white element of the American population. The recent development of an antiracist perception of nonwhites has not overridden this deep tradition of racism because the newer view has affected only the more educated elements of the population. There is still much racism among whites in the United States. This persistent racism has deeply and negatively affected blacks and lowered their self-esteem, even though many are starting to benefit from the end of segregation and from the protection of their civil liberties, which began in the 1960s. The process of racial integration in the full sense of the term—socially, economically, and culturally—will take a long time: beyond the existence of racism, beyond the time when blacks retain the scars of lowered self-esteem.

The importance of getting rich, of urban civility, and of racism directed toward blacks—all are examples (among many others) of traditions of an economic and social character that are of varying age and durability. They are also good illustrations of the fact that traditions characterize all aspects of human life, not just the political dimension. People should realize that the way they live—especially in its most "settled," unquestioned, and noncontroversial aspects—is a result of many traditions, forged and sustained by our ancestors and ourselves through the generations. We and our forebears made these traditions—political, economic, social, or cultural in character—and we can unmake them if they no longer seem to us to be the best way to live.

This point should be very reassuring. It is important for people to realize that we don't have to do anything we truly don't want to do, even if this realization demystifies to some extent those traditions that are still vital and alive, traditions that we still favor.

II

HISTORIANS AND NATIONS

4

The True Nature of Nations and Nationalism

Modern nationalism,[1] which I define as all the manifestations of a particular citizenry's identification with and loyalty to its nation, originated in the western part of Europe. A distinctive convergence of (1) seemingly well-defined cultures (language, art, philosophy), (2) ethnic purity (long-term tribal inbreeding that produced, among others, the modern English, French, or Spanish), and (3) durable national political systems (which emerged out of earlier dynastic states)—all resulted in a rare overlayering of significant aspects of life for the inhabitants of the nations of Western Europe. Especially after the eighteenth century, nationalism became increasingly powerful among these populations, heightening their sense of distinctiveness. People elsewhere on the continent became similarly nationalistic during the course of the nineteenth and early twentieth centuries, as first city-states merged in Central Europe and then empires collapsed in Eastern Europe. Nationalism was exported around the globe as a legacy of European colonialism, when politically independent people in the Americas, Asia, and Africa copied Europe's political ways, established their own nations, and tried to become nationalistic as well.

The emergence of a globe-girdling political system of nation-states (with membership in the United Nations)[2] is the most astonishing instance of the Western domination of the world. It has been far more successful than Western efforts to export Christianity, although, with the collapse of communist governments and their command economies, capitalism may yet encompass the globe as well. Since the effective end of formal, political colonization, virtually everyone on earth is a citizen of a nation-state. The power of both national governments and nationalism has been a worldwide phenomenon of great and explosive impact in our century.

A brief chronology reveals how nation-states have attained a global scope since the late eighteenth century. The "Americans" rebelled during the 1770s, dismembering the British Empire in the process and creating the first modern as well as first ethnically and racially mixed nation. Spanish colonists in South and Central America similarly rebelled during the 1810s, greatly diminishing the Spanish Empire through the establishment of many ethnically and racially varied nations in Latin America during the years thereafter. In the 1860s and 1870s, the Italians and the Germans, hitherto scattered through many local political entities, achieved political union. In Asia, independent Japan and China effectively became nations with the restoration of one empire in 1868 (in the case of Japan) and with the collapse of another empire in 1911 (in the case of China).[3]

By the late nineteenth century, varied ethnic-linguistic-religious groupings sought nationhood within the Austro-Hungarian and Ottoman Empires, and some of these groups either partially or fully achieved their goal as a result of the peace settlement following World War I. After World War II, national liberation movements emerged in colonial Africa and Asia. Some were successful in creating multitribal or ethnically plural nations whose tribally and ethnically insensitive boundaries generally remained those that various European powers had earlier created for their colonies.[4] More recently, nationalist groups have developed secessionist movements in successful efforts to break away from nations (such as the Soviet Union,[5] Yugoslavia, and Czechoslovakia) with populations of a varied ethnic composition. These nationalists groups have taken further the process of nation-building based on ethnicity that had originated after World War I. Throughout all these years, there have always been more nationalist groups in existence than there have been those who have successfully set up their own nations.

Whether fostered by powerful elites, an intelligentsia, broad-gauged popular movements, or combinations of the three, the growth of nationalism was linked to the belief that a common national past binds together all the citizens of a nation. This belief in a common past involved varying amounts of distortion and invention and an exaggerated sense of unity and distinctiveness.[6] Nationalism, from its inception, has taken on many forms and shapes—sometimes popular (as in Western Europe) and other times authoritarian (as in Eastern Europe and Asia); sometimes linked (as in Britain) to the individual and his or her freedom and other times to the collective community (as in France); sometimes born of positive sentiments about the nation (as in Britain) and other times out of hostility toward powerful neighboring nations (as in Central and Eastern Europe); and sometimes based on religious or wartime rivalries of long duration (Britain and France).[7]

The whole process of nation-building has been intricately interconnected with empire. In Western Europe and Asia, nationalism was fostered in a symbiotic relationship to empire in two ways. One took the form of a negative reaction on a national basis to imperial control from afar (as in the case of France's adverse response to the Hapsburgs and their dominion over much of Europe). The other took the form of an internally positive reaction to the growth of a nation's own empire in its rivalry with other imperial centers (as in the case of the nationalistic/imperialistic fervor created within Britain and France and, later, Japan and Germany in response to the growth of empire based in those nations).

Nationalist movements beyond those that developed in the earliest nations have typically been led by what Benedict Anderson has called colonial creoles—elite groups whose pilgrimage or journey to power has been confined to the political dominions of metropoles (or seats of empire).[8] These provincial leaders have eventually copied the ways of their political masters and created nations of their own, usually contained within boundaries already established during the colonial era. These nationalist movements were also intensely, passionately antiforeign, and had as their goal the ending of Western domination in the form of political control, economic exploitation, and racial superiority.[9] Thus, the elites of the newer nations were profoundly schizophrenic in their attitude toward their erstwhile colonial masters. Ironically, although many of the "national liberation" movements of the twentieth century have been communist, and thus theoretically internationalist in their long-term interests, in reality such movements have been thoroughly nationalistic in character.

Nations are "imagined communities" (in Anderson's felicitous phrase), as indeed are all human groups beyond kinship groupings and quite small local communities. They are imagined in the sense that individual citizens cannot know more than a small fraction of their fellow citizens, but can imagine their existence. Modern forms of communication—at first printed books, magazines, and newspapers, and, more recently, radio and television—have greatly facilitated this process.

In the extremely messy and overlapping manner that characterizes all large historical developments, nations have come to replace both wide-ranging religious communities (sometimes bound by linguistic unity, as in the case of Christianity and Latin) and dynastic states (with their divinely sanctioned and sovereign monarchs) with large entities to which masses of human beings give their ultimate loyalty.[10] At the heart of the nationalist sentiment generated by each national political group since the eighteenth century is the belief that the citizens of each nation are distinctive in their history and, indeed, in all aspects of their life. "Our" group is "our" nation, and "we" are different in our identity—both historically and currently—from all "others."

The swift emergence of the nation-state system and the nationalism it has spawned is, historically, a remarkable development. Though now universal, the only people in reality who approached the kind of distinctiveness and uniqueness that nationalism presumes were those who generated the phenomenon in the first place—most notably the British, the French, and the Spanish. And even there, not all significant aspects of life were effectively "nationalized." Both the economy and religion—capitalism and Christianity—remained persistently supranational in character. Even ethnic purity was diluted by the presence of the Welsh and the Scots in Britain, the Bretons in France, and the Basques and Catalans in Spain.

Elsewhere, nationalism and genuine distinctiveness have overlain one another far less frequently. Nations have either shared languages with other nations or have embraced varying degrees of regional dialects or linguistic forms. Nations have rarely been ethnically pure. They have usually encompassed several "ethnic" groupings in their populations. In some cases, one such group has predominated and achieved a generalized "cultural" dominance, but in other cases, there has been a pervasive ethnic plurality.[11] Indeed, in many instances in the modern world minority ethnic groups within nations have perceived themselves to be a people with higher claims on their members' identity and allegiance than the nation itself. Sometimes such groups have sought to establish or in fact have established their own nations. In other cases, ethnically defined peoples, who have been divided into political entities either larger or smaller than the groups themselves, have gone on to establish nations of their own.

Nations have rarely contained economic activity that has been sharply distinctive from that of adjoining territories. Although governments have created currencies, developed trading regulations with other nations, regulated domestic economic activity in various ways, and indeed sometimes (as in communist states) directly "owned" economic entities, the basic patterns of economic life have seldom coincided with political boundaries.[12] There have been state churches, but almost never have there been religious groupings whose geographic configurations have fitted nations perfectly. Usually, religious sects either have extended beyond such territories or have been contained within them. Rarely have artistic forms, particular kinds of philosophical or theological inquiry, or popularly held values and beliefs been confined for long within national borders.[13]

The fact is that human groupings have assumed a vast variety of forms. All human beings belong to various groups with whom they identify simultaneously, sometimes harmoniously and complementarily so, but at other times conflictually, because of the stresses and strains and contradictions and dilemmas that multiple identifications naturally produce. National groupings have never been the only significant form of group identification for individuals anywhere at any time. Age, gender, sexuality, occupation, class, ethnicity, race, language, and (religious) beliefs are other significant bases for human identity. What has developed, however, particularly since the late nineteenth century, among national groups in the more substantial and durable nation states is a deeply engrained and widely shared habit of viewing the past as if all the dimensions of human life have in fact assumed national configurations.

Citizens of modern nations have typically invested their states with "sovereignty," with ultimate claim on their allegiance. They have sometimes allowed their national political identity to overshadow all other forms of identity. People routinely refer to national societies—American, Canadian, British, French, German—as if their national group by itself creates a wholly distinctive way of living. The emergent power of modern nationalism everywhere in the world is a difficult phenomenon to explain unless one recognizes the either willful or unwitting distortions of reality that have been involved whenever national governments and their citizens have tried to generate identification with and loyalty to an exaggeratedly distinctive "national life."

Such national populations have been greatly aided in this process by the existence of fixed borders (unless augmented or diminished by political action) around precisely defined territories, quite unlike the flux and imprecision of the hunting and fishing territories of the tribal groupings that nations have superceded in every part of the globe. Such "fixity" of territory has made it easier for citizenries to think in terms of a specific geographic space that automatically defines the extent of every aspect of "national" life. The fact is that every dimension of human life has its own shape and size and territory. All these dimensions are different from one another, and all are more akin to the indeterminacy of tribal territories than to the precision and fixity of the borders of political states, which have an unusually static, fixed character to their shape.

The perceptions that nationalism has created have been powerful forms of social reality for the groups of citizens so affected. What appears as distortion and exaggeration to the dispassionate observer are deep-seated truths to the ordinary inhabitants of well-developed nations, the historically derived myths and symbols and shared experiences, whether calamitous or triumphant, of a people. The truths resulting from nationalistic fervor can be held with enormous tenacity and can be extremely durable. They lay at the heart of a people's identity. And Americans have been as much affected by nationalism as any other national group in the modern world.

In the case of my own "field" of American history, the true nature of nationhood and nationalism can be clearly seen, I believe. In the portion of North America settled and developed by European migrants and their descendants which, following political independence in the 1780s, became the American nation, nationalism was created all at once during a violent, revolutionary birth.[14]   As citizens of the first modern nation to be established outside Europe, Americans became dedicated to the proposition that theirs was a special nation whose purpose, as the Declaration of Independence adumbrated, was to expand and perfect liberty and, more generally, to provide a setting in which the finest European ideals could find full fruition. America was to be a perfected Europe: The heartland of Western civilization was old and corrupt; America would replenish and extend European ways.

During the nineteenth century, annual Independence Day celebrations turned into a national rite of self-justification.[15] However, the development of a powerful and durable American nationalism was a drawn-out and faltering process, given the pervasively decentralized way Americans settled and lived. Without potent national institutions, without a center or focal point for national life, it was possible in the 1860s for a significant portion of the population to allow its identification with and loyalty to region to override nationalist sentiment to the point that it supported the dismemberment of the political system and the subsequent fighting of a major civil war.[16]

But nationalism revived after the 1870s. At its heart, as earlier, was the sense that America was unique and separate and superior to the motherland. Since the late nineteenth century, nationalism has been a deep-seated, powerful basis for an "American" identity. Basing their nationalist sentiments on what until the 1970s was an increasingly powerful nation-state, Americans have usually had a strong sense that their ever-mightier country was special and distinctive and worthy of identifying with in every dimension of their lives.[17]

But historical realities have been quite different. Americans have not fulfilled European ideals: their historical record abounds in contradiction, reflecting an ongoing coexistence between various forms of freedom and slavery, liberty and tyranny, equality and inequality, hierarchy and mobility. In this respect, Americans haven't been much different from people in other parts of the world and at other times in the human past. Neither have they been especially distinctive in their reformist efforts to close the gap between their ideals and their social reality; nor are they in any sense unique in regarding themselves as a "special" people, as a glance at the British, French, German, Russian, Chinese, or Japanese pasts reveals.

Furthermore, American life has born the impress of its British colonial origins. Americans, of course, do not speak or write in their own language, and their legal and political systems evolved out of a larger eighteenth-century British political world. "America" has shared modern Europe's cultural, religious, and ethnic variety, as well as that continent's underlying unity—its inclusive Christianity and capitalism, its emergent liberalism, its industrial and technological orientation.

What was distinctive about America was that, in the New World, transplanted Europeans cleansed themselves of feudalism, monarchy, and aristocracy, all of which, in various forms, continued to be a significant part of European life until the nineteenth or twentieth centuries. At the same time, the colonists added slavery, or racial castes, to their social system, thus adding a new "bottom" to their European-derived society while losing that society's aristocratic "top."

What was also different about European North American settlements was that the religious and ethnic or national groups that have until recently been geographically discrete and separate in Europe, quickly became spacially amalgamated in North America. Adherents of Christian sects that occupied particular geographic areas in Europe often moved into close proximity to one another within particular local communities or rural neighborhoods in North America. Similarly, European national and ethnic groups, together with their descendants, moved into ever closer residential configurations, eventually integrating and intermarrying. In the process, they created an ingathering of European peoples (the same way that slaves from different African tribes created a new amalgamation of Afro-Americans), just as ancient tribes in Europe itself, through cross-breeding, had produced the modern English, French, or Germans.

American republicanism, with its absence of monarchy and hereditary aristocracy, significantly distinguished the United States from most European states until the twentieth century. But this modern form of republicanism rather quickly became a phenomenon with hemispheric dimensions when rebellious Spanish colonists tried to adopt the American model while establishing independent nations after their successful early nineteenth-century rebellions.

Furthermore, the range of powers and the overall functions of government at all levels were quite similar in Europe and America throughout this period. America's enlarged electorates, mass political parties, and title-less officeholders seemed quite distinctive from the late eighteenth to the late nineteenth century. During the twentieth century, the citizens of a growing number of nations have barred monarchs and aristocrats from performing a significant political role as they have either developed increasingly democratic political arrangements or, at times, subjected themselves to new forms of autocratic, though nonaristocratic, governments. Even during the eighteenth and nineteenth centuries, however, polities all over the Europeanized world based government to some extent on the principle of popular representation. And, in this century, welfare-capitalist states have been created throughout the Western world.

Instead of a stratified society that included inherited aristocratic rankings, American white men (and, until recently, only white men) have relied on the accumulation of wealth garnered from a resourceful land both as a basis for frequent social and geographic mobility—and as a new arbiter of social status. Since the nineteenth century, however, aristocratic wealth and power in Europe have gradually given way to those who have amassed both without benefit of titles. During the nineteenth and twentieth centuries, the coexistence of growing ethnic amalgamation and continued racial enslavement, then segregation, and most recently ghettoization seemed to be a phenomenon distinctive to America. But in this century Europe has at least begun to take on one of those characteristics, as non-Europeans, for various reasons, have started to emigrate to Europe, thus countering an older, outflowing migratory pattern. The result is that Europe's geographically discrete, ethnically defined populations are beginning to be less separate and distinct.

As in other ethnically pluralistic nations, there has been a rather ill-defined core group in America who has enjoyed a wide-ranging domination over the remainder of the population. This ethnic hegemony has been directly linked to the length of residence in North America of particular European settlers and their descendants. One of the most important aspects of ethnicity and race in America, as in many other nations, has been the question of how "American" various groups have been. Those who have perceived themselves as incontestably and fully American have always been considerably fewer in number than the total population of the United States. American nativism has always involved a quest for who and what is American. The naming of particular ethnic and racial groups (before their amalgamation and assimilation) as "hyphenated" Americans is an indication not only of a nativist perception, but also of the ambiguity with which minorities perceive themselves: Are they "American"? Or are they still what they were before coming to America? In this sense, a social definition of who is an American has always been narrower than a political, territorial, geographic one, and the inhabitants of the United States have always been a larger group than "full-blooded" Americans.

The power of nationalism in the United States, as elsewhere, has led Americans and their historians to have a distorted view of historical reality and has fostered an exaggerated sense of American uniqueness for a population that in certain ways has been distinctive, to some extent, for particular periods of time, but in many other ways has not been. It is important that Americans, as well as all the other national groups around the world, try to understand the power that nationalism has to distort historical reality. To be an American is to have a political identity. The ease with which historians apply this political term to other dimensions of life compounds the confusion that laypeople bring to their view of the past.

It is extremely important for academic historians not to assume that a population that has a political identity behaves in distinctive ways in the nonpolitical dimensions of its life. Historians should not use nations (or other political entities) as the basis for their study of particular aspects of the past unless it can clearly be shown that the subjects they wish to study mirror political boundaries. Is something truly "American" in the sense that it characterized the entire population: all localities, all regions, all segments? If not, then the United States should not be used as the unit for study. And even if it can be demonstrated that a particular institution or activity or pattern of behavior was distinctively American in the sense of being essentially the same all over the United States, the question should be asked: Are those distinctions sufficiently basic for the United States as a political entity to be an appropriate basis for study, or should the space and time that a scholar or scholars select be diminished or augmented or disconnected to political boundaries altogether? The fact that a significant element of a politically defined population believes that its life is distinctive or unique does not make its life distinctive or unique. Such a belief is a form of nationalism and is itself a political phenomenon, not a statement of fact.

I am not arguing that nonpolitical historical subjects should never be studied within national political contexts. In the case of the United States, as just indicated, some features of American life were distinctive to some extent and for certain periods of time. The challenge for historians is to make judgments as to what territory and period of time—what scale—is appropriate for them to study a particular phenomenon. Such a scale may or may not involve political boundaries and may in fact involve parts of nations, areas within a single nation, a continent, a hemisphere, or everywhere in the world. The historian's focus should be fixed (like a lens turned until it creates a clear view) at whatever territory and period will best illuminate the overall pattern of whatever subject he or she is studying.

One of the basic reasons why historians choose national contexts for their studies is that nations (governments, national institutions of various kinds) generate records, and leave usable evidence. It takes perseverance to look beyond such categorization and stake out the natural contours of the subject a historian wishes to pursue. Awareness of other, prior scholarship covering other parts of the world (usually other nations) would greatly aid a scholar in this task. But scholars of the United States—historians and social scientists generally—have long focused on American "exceptionalism."[18] Academic historians in particular have exhibited a strong and lasting tendency to study all aspects of life in the United States—not just the political—from an American perspective.

This tendency has been stronger among historians of the United States than among other groups of national historians in the "Westernized" portions of the globe. Europe, Western Civilization (usually without reference to North America or Australasia), Asia, the Far East, South Asia, the Middle East, Africa, Latin America—all are recognized as supranational fields of study. But it is a rare historian who claims that his or her field is North America or the Americas or any other designation that would link the United States to wider geographic territories.[19]

However, it was not a historian, but a sociologist, Seymour Martin Lipset, most notably in *The First New Nation: The United States in Historical and Comparative Perspective* (1963),[20] who made perhaps the most influential study of American exceptionalism. Lipset argued that Americans have embodied a distinctive combination of values that profoundly affect the way they live. Equality and achievement (or opportunity)—not by themselves uniquely American—have been the Americans' tension-filled, compatible/incompatible core values, affecting everything else. Why have Americans had a peculiar value system? Lipset's answer, one that I find unpersuasive, is that Americans share revolutionary and puritanical origins. Lipset places an impossible burden on a political act (the revolution) that left many in opposition or indifferent and that, in any case, can hardly explain a continuous allegiance thereafter to equality and achievement, as Lipset argues. Similarly, a puritanical religiosity, which in Lipset's account of the matter, directly involved a single group (the Puritans) in a single region (New England), and the Calvinism that he claims the Puritans espoused can hardly be said to have characterized the entire population either then or later.

In 1989, Nuffield College in Oxford University sponsored an Anglo-American conference entitled "American Exceptionalism—A Return and Reassessment." In 1991, the papers delivered at that conference were edited by Byron Shafer under the heading *Is America Different?: A New Look at American Exceptionalism.*[21] What is particularly striking about this stocktaking exercise is the unquestioned presumption of its participants that if any evidence at all can be found that demonstrates that life was in any way different in the United States from what it was in other nations, it therefore follows that there was a distinctively "American" way of life, true for Americans everywhere in the nation.

In a renewed effort to find an underlying unity to American exceptionalism, Shafer enlarges Lipset's earlier effort by arguing that individualism, market-making, democratization, and populism are four intertwining, compatible characteristics or values of "American" life that have been so basic that they create a distinctively American pattern in every dimension of human life. Why have these characteristics, which surely are also present in some form among other politically defined populations, been distinctively American in their continuous importance and workable conjunction? Shafer's unsatisfactory explanation is that Americans have been exceptionally diverse both socially and politically.[22]

Both Lipset and Shafer fail to provide persuasive explanations of why Americans should share a peculiar set of values, which, in turn makes every aspect of life in the United States exceptional or different from that of people living in other nations. Another narrower, more precise, measure of American exceptionalism is to ask the question: How different have particular institutions, activities, and patterns of behavior been?

Martin Trow has found, for instance, that American higher education was quite distinctive (all over the United States, public and private) from Europe's in terms of its organizational structure (with lay boards, strong presidents, and a relatively "flat" faculty hierarchy), its relationships to its students (with an emphasis on providing services), and its links to society (with fund-raising, research, and service provisions).[23] But the question not asked is, What other aspects of higher education have been similar to Europe's? For example, how different was the content of what was taught and learned? How different has the curriculum been? Could it be that, even with respect to a subject in which there have been easily identifiable and truly American differences, it might be more revealing to adopt a perspective wider (or narrower) than the United States to understand the historical development of, in this case, postsecondary education?

In another example, Peter Temin argues that industrial capitalism, first developed by the British and later imported by Americans, became distinctive in the United States early in the nineteenth century through the creation of an American System of Manufacturing (based on the assembly-line machine production of interchangeable parts for a given product) and, later in the nineteenth century, through the development of large-scale corporate structures.[24] In the twentieth century, it can be argued that the Americans developed consumerism, an obsession concerning the possession of material goods. None of these innovations was American for long, as Europeans quickly copied the Americans. Similarly, such cultural innovations as skyscraper architecture, jazz, and abstract expressionist and pop art painting, along with such philosophical outlooks as pragmatism, were all regional before becoming national and quickly became international in scope after becoming national. Could it be, then, that, even when there are indisputably American innovations in particular facets of life, given the nature of modern communications and transportation, such innovations have only briefly been solely and distinctively American phenomena?

Ian Tyrrell, in "American Exceptionalism in an Age of International History,"[25] takes issue with the whole notion that the American nation must be presumed to have been significantly different and urges historians of the United States to broaden their focus, to make transnational probings when studying subjects of an economic, environmental, or organizational character, for example. Such historians could more insightfully probe the character of economic, social, and cultural-intellectual development in the United States if they freed themselves from their thraldom to nationalism and the national perspective associated with it. The reality is that the nonpolitical aspects of human life have their own shifting boundaries or territories and do not fit neatly into politically defined areas. By setting up "fields" of historical study based on political entities, national historians have distorted the natural extent of particular forms or patterns of economic, social, and cultural-intellectual activity.

The nonpolitical aspects of human life—such as medicine, science, technology, education, philosophy, religion, recreation and leisure, industry, and agriculture—all have configurations of their own, different from those of a political nature, all affected by government but independent of it. Throughout human history, groups who have created governments have not brought into their political entities a fully distinctive way of living. Human interaction has been far too complicated for a politically defined group to be distinctive in all the other dimensions of its life as well. So, the nonpolitical aspects of life are better understood if they are not studied within politically defined territories.

Freed of the distortions created by their linkage of history and politics, historians everywhere, I believe, could then routinely employ a global perspective as the most revealing basis for deciding how to define their particular slice of our common, human past.

5

The Limitation of National Histories as Fields of Study

It is understandable that historians of the United States have attempted to find historical explanations for various forms of American uniqueness, since most of these historians have been American citizens, and, as such, are as susceptible to the influences of nationalism as other citizens. Indeed, the great bulk of academic scholarship has appeared since the late nineteenth century, from the time nations and nationalism became indisputably major forces of modern life throughout Europe and the Europeanized parts of the world. The citizens of modern nations have believed that their national life is distinctive and different from that of other national groups. These beliefs, though they have involved much distortion and exaggeration, have been a social reality for millions of such citizens, and historians have found it natural to probe what their countrymen have believed to be true about what distinguishes themselves from others. Moreover, the very power of nations makes them a familiar and useful category around which to organize historical study, as does the accessibility of archival material couched in a language already known to native-born scholars.

Academic historians, since their emergence in the late nineteenth century, have been handmaidens of nationalism, providing explanations for the United States' swift emergence as a nation of great power and influence in textbooks and studies assigned to thousands of students in colleges and universities. In the same way, secondary and primary school teachers distilled and simplified such explanations further for millions of school children, so that both groups of students would become better citizens, performing their civic duty by becoming knowledgeable of their nation's past.

Very few teachers—at any level—have questioned the presumption that a survey of "U.S." history is basically a chronology of periodized political change. But teachers and textbook authors alike have been made increasingly uneasy about the great proliferation of scholarship in economic, social, and cultural-intellectual subjects. What exactly is the place of such findings in a survey of U.S. history to be? What, if any, overall interpretation of the American historical experience do such studies suggest?

Efforts since the 1960s to create historiographical syntheses have not been successful. The historians who have been involved in this process have been quite responsive to the burgeoning amount of scholarship dealing with the economic, social, and cultural-intellectual dimensions of American life. But their interpretations have failed to provide either an acceptable context for the inquiries of other historians or a convincing outline that textbook authors have utilized.[1]

There are at least two general reasons why all recent efforts to develop overall syntheses of this kind are, by their nature, incapable of achieving historiographical and interpretive dominance. One relates to developments in the organization of history as a discipline. Since the 1960s, there has been a profusion of (often interdisciplinary) methods and subjects in academic historical inquiry, many of whose practitioners and advocates have formed their own "subspecialties," their own associations and journals, which in turn has led to an increasing ignorance of the "whole" field on the part of still presumably American historians. Those who have studied such subjects as blacks, women, Indians, immigrants, the family, cities, recreation and sport, popular culture and folklore, medicine and science, and demography have all organized in this manner.

The frequently interdisciplinary character of such scholarship has led to cross-disciplinary institutes, programs, appointments, and course offerings. History departments have sometimes ignored traditional fields such as U.S. history in their hiring, basing appointments on subject rather than geographical areas. Accompanying the proliferation of subspecialties has been a corresponding subdivision of American history into journals specializing in the colonial period (the *William and Mary Quarterly*) and the early republic, as well as into texts confined to periods (such as the twentieth century or even since World War II) or to aspects of the field (such as U.S. economic, diplomatic, intellectual, or religious history).

Since the 1960s it has become increasingly apparent that there has been an enormous growth in specialization among those still nominally called American historians. As a consequence, professors of American history teach courses far broader than their area of scholarship. In the process, they are relying increasingly, and (I will argue) vainly, on textbook authors and synthesizers to integrate their published work into a field that has lost much of the coherence it appeared to have before the emergence of this growing array of subspecialties in the newer areas of research within the nonpolitical aspects of the past.

An even more important explanation for the failure of recent textbook authors and historiographers to successfully develop a new synthesis relates to something that I believe inheres in the nature of history itself, namely, that the nonpolitical aspects of American (or any other "national") life can be examined with more insight from perspectives either larger or smaller, but in either case, different from national and political ones.

It is also the case that those identified (and studied historically) as Americans were organized into families and local, state, and regional communities in ways far more important than the ways they were associated in a national context—before the twentieth century. Furthermore, within the context of the American political system, the national government was created in 1787–1788 as a government of defined and limited authority. Significant aspects of American life either were a legitimate concern of state and local government in a decentralized federal structure or were beyond the ambit of constitutionally derived authority altogether.[2]

It is also true, however, that from the eighteenth to the twentieth century governmental power has expanded, at all levels, and in the twentieth century, especially at the national level. Politicians have found constitutional justification for what it has been politically desirable to do. Thus, such newer areas of governmental activity as social welfare, health, science, medicine, the environment, and culture have emerged.[3] By the late nineteenth century, the capacity and desire of Americans to organize on a national basis became unmistakable. Since then, economic corporations have created continent-wide forms of financing, producing, transporting, and selling consumer products of ever increasing variety. Labor and farmers' unions; financial, industrial, and commercial associations; professional, scientific, medical, and academic organizations; social clubs; and "lobbies" or advocacy agencies of many kinds—all attest to the extent to which Americans have organized nationally since the nineteenth century.

But the fact remains that nonpolitical phenomena have changing configurations and territories of their own. The economic, social, and cultural-intellectual aspects of human life do not fit exactly within political boundaries, despite the efforts of Americans and other national groups to organize various aspects of their lives along national lines. These efforts have not, by themselves, made economic social cultural intellectual life in the United States (and in other nations) distinctive and different from what it is or has been in the rest of the world. And, though affected, influenced, regulated, or even directed by government, these other aspects of life are not political phenomena. They have a definition, a life, an integrity of their own. They can be studied as they interact with government, as they become matters of political discussion or action.

In this sense, a politically focused survey of the American past can legitimately become as wide as the concerns of the political community itself. But to study, say, religion, culture, science, technology, philosophy, recreation, industry, and agriculture from the standpoint of political interaction is hugely different from studying these phenomena on their own terms. If anyone studying the American past confronts such discrete dimensions of human life only as they become matters of governmental/political activity, then he or she severely limits his or her understanding.

Any nonpolitical aspect of life may involve government or have a public aspect and can be studied from a political perspective. Such subjects also exist independently of government and need to be examined on their own terms, within their own territories, from their own perspective. The best and most effective way to do this is for historians to ignore political boundaries as they demarcate the geographic extent of the nonpolitically defined subjects being studied. It is this basic aspect of historical reality that historians who are synthesizers have usually ignored.

With very few exceptions, those academic historians who have produced influential or important syntheses of various aspects of American life have not been concerned about the great distortion that results from trying to fit the nonpolitical aspects of human life into politically defined territories. Because their field of history is American history and because they have learned to perceive the past as something capable of being studied—in all its dimensions—in a fixed, given American political context, such synthesizers have summarized and interpreted in nationally defined and confined accounts the great outpouring of scholarly writing that a growing army of specialists have produced in recent decades.

Themselves imbued with nationalism, these historians, like most other Americans, presume that there is a distinctive American way in every aspect of life beyond the political one. Nationalism has colored the perception that American citizens, including their historical synthesizers, have of all aspects of life in the United States. Nationalism has affected the way Americans of all descriptions perceive economic, social, and cultural-intellectual phenomena, all of which, they believe, can naturally, automatically, and most meaningfully be studied within a national context. But what I want to argue here is that historians can more insightfully and meaningfully study the nonpolitical aspects of the past from contexts that vary in size and scope and that are "unlinked" to political territories, especially national ones.[4]

Examples abound. For instance, family life can be probed from either a local or regional or a civilizational or even a global context more revealingly than from an "American" or a national context.[5] Scholars have quite routinely studied the family in local or regional contexts, but Philip Greven's plea that family life be studied in a world-embracing context has gone largely unheeded.[6] Similarly, towns and cities can best be investigated in either a local/regional or a transnational setting. Urbanization has much larger dimensions than American ones and much greater local or regional variations than scholarly generalizations based on the United States alone have revealed.[7] Kenneth Lockridge's insistence that American towns be examined in the widest possible context has largely been ignored.[8]

Even well-studied social phenomena—such as race and gender, immigration and ethnicity, and class—greatly benefit from being studied in both much narrower and much wider contexts. There have been a number of studies of slavery in particular localities and states within the United States. But slavery was not, of course, a uniquely American phenomenon, unless "American" is given a larger, and more accurate, hemispheric definition. Some of the most influential studies of slavery have profited from their author's awareness of this fact.[9] Racial slavery and segregation was an experience American blacks have shared with other blacks.[10]

Women's distinctive and inferior position has been essentially the same in all the major civilizations of the world, and has largely been ignored by those who have written the rapidly growing volume of studies on women's history in the United States, which is usually presented either in national or much more localized contexts.[11] Immigration and the presence of ethnic groups both within and beyond national political boundaries are a global phenomenon and, more particularly, are characteristics of the expansion of European civilization around the world. But the international aspect of these phenomena is not learned from the scholarship on the history of American immigration and ethnicity, although many studies of these subjects have been made in local or regional contexts.[12]

The development of a middle-class culture or way of life is as broad as Western civilization, not something whose characteristics are most revealingly probed within an American context, as many scholars have in fact done in their studies of various aspects of middle-class life. Similarly, the poor and the laboring or working classes (in spite of Marxist formulations) have rarely been investigated in contexts that extend beyond the United States. The American upper class—based on wealth generated from agricultural, commercial, financial, or industrial sources—can be revealingly studied from the perspective of elites around the world, as part of a global phenomenon in which small groups have amassed great wealth and wielded enormous power throughout human history, either on the basis of heredity or talent, or both. But these considerations are largely absent from the relevant scholarship, which has instead exhibited a tendency to be focused on localities and regions within the United States and to involve generalizations for a presumably national phenomenon based on the study of local groups.[13]

Although economic and religious historians have written much about the "national" or American economy and the various Christian denominations within the United States, the stubborn fact remains that capitalism and Christianity are economic and religious phenomena with vast transnational dimensions, and it matters more that an economic firm is a corporation (not an "American" one) or that a church is a Christian one (not an "American" one).[14] Science and medicine are obvious examples of a subject in need of a nonpolitical definition. To provide a national basis for an activity whose practitioners have usually sought universal uniformity is to create largely artificial distinctions, in spite of scholarly efforts to focus on American science and medicine.[15]

Particular forms of sport and recreation and leisure-time activities have spread to large areas of the globe, a development not usually emphasized by the growing number of those who have written on these phenomena in an American context.[16] Athletic teams competing on behalf of particular towns, cities, counties, states, and the United States itself is another example of political communities generating loyalty and identity among their inhabitants and is not a meaningful basis for studying the development of a given sport.

All the major forms of artistic activity—music, painting, sculpture, dance, architecture, fiction, poetry—much as cultural historians have tried to fit them into American national political boundaries, remain resistant to such treatment, for cultural forms have extended over wide areas of the globe, as well as exhibiting enormous local and regional variations within nations.[17] The Americanness of particular artists and art forms—that is, the national qualities and characteristics of artistic works and their creators—is typically something that cultural historians can presume rather than demonstrate. How do the creations of artists of any kind embody the spirit or temperament of the entire population of a nation, with its usual ethnic variety, class structure, and gender distinctions?

Despite continuous pleas from cultural nationalists that there should be a distinctive American culture, until the twentieth century, art in America was on the cultural periphery or frontier of Europe, and art forms that had been nurtured and defined in Europe were regularly copied by American artists, even while they drew on materials and settings from within America. Occasionally, there were mavericks who, perhaps because they were less beholden to tradition than European artists generally were, created fresh forms of art (Edgar Allan Poe's horror and detective stories, Walt Whitman's free verse, Louis Sullivan's skyscrapers). By the twentieth century, when new art forms (such as jazz and rock music, abstract expressionist and pop art) were created in the United States, they relatively quickly moved beyond America's national boundaries.

Similarly, philosophy, though sometimes initially encased in national languages, as in parts of Europe, has amply displayed itself in larger contexts, with much evidence of cross-fertilization and transnational influences, although the works of intellectual historians usually do not focus on such matters.[18] Within the American national context, in the case of political philosophy, both the philosophical justification for the colonial rebellion of 1775–1781 and the philosophical basis for the Constitution of 1787 were heavily derivative of British or, more generally, European viewpoints. As for metaphysical thought in America, even pragmatism, though it originated within the United States, has competed with other, European-derived philosophical viewpoints for intellectual dominance.[19]

Both Americans themselves and foreign observers have ascribed to the inhabitants of the United States a distinctive national character, a unique blend of characteristics, a particular group profile. But as was the case with ideas and art, I believe it is inaccurate to claim that a politically defined population, especially with the looseness and variety of the Americans, "embodies" particular traits. Who has embraced them? Has everyone who has lived in the territory, in its various regions and localities? Have blacks, Native Americans, women, children, the insane, criminals, the poor, the very rich? Why should people who have formed their own political entity and who have developed an identity with and loyalty to that entity (that is, who are nationalistic) necessarily behave in a distinctive manner?

Nationalistic as they have been, Americans have presumed that they have had a national character. Outside observers have similarly focused on distinctive traits that they believe they have noticed while they were traveling in the United States or while they encountered Americans traveling abroad. Such observers, naturally responsive to the widespread practice of identifying persons by their national citizenship, have had a deeply engrained tendency to ascribe to all Americans what they've noticed in particular Americans. (The strangeness and apartness that exist whenever these observers or those they've observed have been outside their "home" territory have only heightened this proclivity to generalize.) In this way, both domestic and foreign observers produce stereotypes, caricatures, and inaccurate generalizations about the behavior of either "us" or "them," either one's fellow Americans or those others who are Americans. The ease with which people erroneously ascribe a national character to Americans and other politically defined groups is yet another example of the effect of a globally pervasive nationalism.[20]

Textbook authors and other synthesizers have usually obscured the fact that the people repeatedly studied in their guise as U.S. citizens have had—as have all human beings in the past—multiple, simultaneously held identities, loyalties, and allegiances—all important, arguably all as fundamental as their national political one. Americans have also been defined by age, gender, sexuality, occupation, class, race, ethnicity, language, and (religious) beliefs and have been members of local, state, and regional communities. Each of these factors, it can be argued, is as valid a basis for grouping for purposes of historical study as their national political affiliation has been.

But these alternative bases for historical study do not naturally form into groupings along national political lines, any more than, say, linguistic, artistic, scientific, philosophical, religious, educational, economic, social, or geographic bases do for historical study. Even the American nation benefits from comparative study with other nations as to its basic role, form, and function in the lives of its citizens.[21]

Indeed, a significant level of world government is likely to appear as a result of the increasingly global pattern of many aspects of human life. The emergence of such a world government would involve the surrender of national political sovereignty and would probably come either as a result of the development of supranational, continental government out of prior economic unions (such as the Common Market in Europe) or as the consequence of continental or even hemispheric political associations (such as the Organization of African Unity or the Organization of American States). Or the United Nations itself might evolve into a world government with sovereign powers. (An analogy would be the American states under the Articles of Confederation changing into the American nation under the Constitution.) Human rights groups checking for infractions of civil liberties, international observers monitoring elections, the International Monetary Fund or the World Bank making loans contingent on economic "performance"—all are indications that agencies with a global reach are already affecting the activities of national governments.

Comparative history as an approach to historical study greatly benefits from careful definition. If the comparisons to be made are directly between nation-states, then the subject being dealt with either should be defined as political—that is, focused on the activities of the government or the electorate—or should be studied strictly from a political perspective. Otherwise, economic, social, cultural, or intellectual subjects, because they are not usually coterminous with political boundaries, benefit from geographic comparisons that are not defined politically at all.[22]

Americans, like other national political groups, have had a distorted view of both the past and the present as a result of their deeply engrained habit of observing life from a national perspective. In their minds, political boundaries have become deep grooves across the face of the globe. Like moats or barriers, they are felt to separate life (in all its aspects) in one nation from that in all others. Geography itself is often perceived in terms of political boundaries rather than in its own natural configurations. For example, in North America, the Rocky Mountains and the Great Plains become the Canadian or American Rockies or Plains. The great plain of Europe becomes the plains of France, Germany, Poland, or Russia. The Alps become the Swiss or Italian or the Austrian Alps.

Americans—not just ordinary Americans, but critics, observers, commentators, journalists, group leaders, the most articulate participants in particular aspects of life in America—automatically think of American science and medicine, the American economy, American sports leagues, American art, American society, and so on—whether or not it would be more meaningful and revealing to observe these phenomena from other, wider or narrower contexts or perspectives. I believe that it is important that historians take the lead and henceforth study the past on the basis of "movable contexts," demarcating the scope of their inquiries with reference to what both prior study and current reflections suggest are the natural parameters or the geographical extent of the subject to be investigated.

Historians bear a special responsibility for developing among the populace at large a powerful connection between historical study and the nation-state, between history and past politics. Academic historical writing emerged in a symbiotic relationship to the creation and development of nations and nationalism. Scholars based their fields of study on their nation-states and have routinely generalized about all aspects of life on the basis of nations or other political entities. But they now have an opportunity to unlink the deeply engrained habit of studying the past primarily through the perspective of national groups and political entities.

I am arguing that recent efforts to produce textual and historiographical syntheses of the American past have not been successful because the burgeoning volume of academic scholarship focused on the nonpolitical aspects of life cannot be satisfactorily organized on a national or American basis.

It is also the case, however, that some national groups, the Americans among them, continue to have a powerful sense of identity, and it is undoubtedly the case that there will continue to be historians who will present accounts of the American past because of its continued significance as an historical subject.

In the future, however, synthesizers who seek to provide a general account of life in the United States and its colonial antecedents should offer their interpretations of economic, social, or cultural-intellectual life as instances of life in America, rather than probings of the American economy, society, culture, and thought. *American* is a political prefix, whereas the term *life in America* suggests that nonpolitical phenomena have a shape, an extent, a place of their own, and have not and do not coincide with politically defined territories, even though a given synthesizer has confined his or her study to that particular kind of entity. Therefore, such synthesizers should be particularly sensitive and clear whenever the patterns of economic, social, and cultural-intellectual life in the United States reveal local or regional variations or exhibit a "territoriality" greater than the nation itself.

Even though their ongoing focus is on the nation, these scholars should also make it clear that the human beings they are studying in their guise as citizens of a nation—as "Americans"—all had multiple identities that they held simultaneously with their national political one, a situation that creates multiple perspectives from which their lives can and should be examined by historians and their readers and students. Synthesizers should explore these other forms of identity alongside the political ones.

Future accounts of the American historical experience should also contain units that deal with each aspect of life in America in overlapping but distinctive time frames. Periodization that makes sense for political life does not make sense for economic or social or cultural-intellectual life, simply because change does not occur in lockstep fashion. For example, economic developments have usually been of a longer term character than political ones, suggesting quite a different chronology; social and cultural evolution are similarly autonomous and should be accorded their own periodization. There should be one overall chronology in such textual or analytical accounts, with units on each aspect of life in a given sequence or order, each with its own staggered but overlapping dates.[23]

All these changes would result in the production of syntheses of the American past that would be much more complicated than textual accounts have been. However, I believe that such syntheses would also be far more reflective of what current scholarship suggests are feasible ways of generalizing about national groups. These new accounts would contain multiple vectors or framings and would be multiperspectival in character and thus be more sophisticated renderings of their subject than has been the case. But I believe that such syntheses would be vastly more valuable than the formulaic texts that historians have produced without significant change since the 1920s.

Future synthesizers of the American past should proceed with an awareness that inquiries into a world divided into nation-states are largely political in nature—nations are political entities. Throughout human history, groups have been creating their own political entities. But groups with a distinctive political identity have not typically been distinctive in other ways as well, in spite of their continuous efforts to convince themselves and others that all aspects of their lives have been and are different or unique. Human interaction has been far too complex and varied for there to have been a continuous "overlayering" between the political and the other aspects of these groups' lives. This has been the case from the time of the earliest human civilizations, from the time when nomadic tribes attacked settled agricultural groups.

Despite the historic and ongoing efforts of citizens to discern, nurture, or protect presumed national distinctiveness or uniqueness in all areas of life, and despite the engrained tendency of academic historians to study everything in modern history from within national perspectives, the reality is that the world's population has historically assumed different configurations and boundaries and definitions, depending on the aspect of human life being investigated. The public should be made aware that the past can be meaningfully viewed from many perspectives, and not just from that of their nation-state.

The popular proclivity for seeing all of history from a governmental and national viewpoint is another byproduct of nationalism. Individuals who live in the United States should recognize that they have multiple identities that project themselves onto the past in different ways and with varying demographic and geographic outlines. Every human being is identified by his or her age, gender, sexuality, occupation, class, ethnicity, race, language, and (religious) belief, as well as by citizenship, and all are the basis for important forms of human groupings.

The fostering of national identity and loyalty should no longer be the chief effect of history as taught and studied in the schools. Children and adolescents will understand the human past only when they are freed of such nationalistic compartmentalization, which has been both a form of intellectual imprisonment and a perceptual distortion.

The best way to change the public's way of seeing history is for economic, social, and cultural-intellectual historians themselves to be trained outside the boundaries of "national" fields. History departments should be encouraged to hire such historians without reference to national fields of study. Journals unconfined to national contexts—such as the *Journal of Social History*, the *Journal of Family History*, and the *Journal of Women's History*—should be given the resources to flourish. University and college courses with a nonpolitical focus should be enthusiastically supported.

It is time for historians to free themselves from their enthrallment to nationalism, to the distorting power of a force in modern life that has seriously diminished our capacity to understand our common, human past.[24]

III

HISTORIANS AND LOCAL COMMUNITIES

6

"Prehistorical" Definitions of Local Communities

People are natural empiricists: that is, they naturally focus on particular things, not categories of things. Those trained to think academically can become comfortable with categories, but categories are rational, self-conscious creations of the human mind. Most people are not comfortable thinking about such concepts as community, the concept that has been the basis for the way that academic historians have organized the past for purposes of study. But most people are interested in such cities as New York, not in cities generally, in such towns as Deerfield, Massachusetts, not in towns generally, and in such nations as the United States of America, not in nations generally. Scholars, by contrast, are trained to study general phenomena, to examine particular things for their value as illustrations or evidence of general phenomena.

I've already indicated that academic historians have organized their fields of study on the basis of political entities, whether empires, nations, provinces (or states), or city-states. This basis for organizing humanity's past is inherently flawed, basically because the other, nonpolitical aspects of human life have not assumed the same shape as politically defined territories. I would like now to focus on local communities, the places where people actually live, that people occupy in a way they cannot dwell in a province or a nation or an empire, those larger, invisible communities that have nonetheless evoked strong forms of loyalty and identification. Academic historians have been as concerned to define local communities as they have to define any other form of community that they've studied. A ceaseless quest to reach an ever-elusive consensus on definition is, indeed, a hallmark of academic study, a quest that is a natural corollary of the scholarly focus on categories of human phenomena.

In what follows, I am going to concentrate on local communities in the United States because my teaching and scholarship have been confined to that field of study. Nonetheless, it is important to note that nothing makes towns and cities within the United States a natural unit of study beyond the fact that all such local communities are part of a particular federal political system. All levels of government—local, state, and federal—within this system have interacted in various ways. Thus, it makes sense to study local communities in the United States from a political perspective, but from no other. There is nothing beyond politics that makes all such communities "American." There is nothing distinctive about American towns and cities in an economic, social, or cultural-intellectual sense; there is nothing that makes these communities—all together, everywhere in the continent-wide nation—different from towns and cities in Canada or Britain or France or Germany or Spain or Italy or any other nation. And yet, those scholars who have thus far tried to generalize about such communities in the United States have not been aware of the limited basis on which it makes sense to study American towns and cities as a unit.

The first historians who dealt with local communities in the United States were amateurs who, with few exceptions, published all the local histories we have, at least until the mid-twentieth century. For over a century, from the 1820s to the 1930s, amateurs dominated the field of local historical writing while an emergent academic profession focused its study elsewhere, on thin slices of national political life. As I've argued in *Families and Communities* (1974) and *Keepers of Our Past* (1988), these amateur local historians concentrated on the level of community that mattered most to those living in the United States. Indeed, their domination coincided roughly with the period that these local communities were themselves the dominant level of community.

It is ironic that these empirically minded amateurs, out of either love or hope of commercial gain, focused their efforts on that which was near and familiar. In retrospect, we can now see that they chose the most important level of community to examine, while an increasingly analytically minded professoriate became overwhelmingly concerned about the emergence of the United States as a nation, concerned, that is, about a fledgling political entity that until the 1930s was less important than the regions, states, or local communities within it. It's as if innocent amateurs had a natural sense of what was most important, while knowledgeable professionals became unwitting handmaidens of nationalism, "boosting" the United States through texts and courses offered to students, but also studying and writing about a nation whose past was relatively insignificant to the very people who inhabited the large part of the North American continent embraced by the United States.

The amateur historians who became involved with recovering and preserving the past of their local communities did not in any significant way analyze, interpret, conceptualize, or generalize about their subject. In that respect, they were no different from those who subscribed to their publications. But they were distinctive in the amount of labor and time they put into their study of their communities' past and present. The typical amateur was a member of the local elite, someone who identified strongly with his town or city, usually because his own family was long associated with it and had attained prominence of some kind within it. These amateurs acted, as the term connotes, out of love for their community. To them, their town or city had a past and a present and undoubtedly a future that they were proud of. They felt that it was well worth the expenditure of the years of effort that it took them to produce what they hoped would be long-lasting publications of various kinds.

In their accounts or records of their town's or city's achievement, they made family and community mesh: one was an extension of the other. They weren't interested in everyone who happened to live in their community. The families they wrote sketches of were prominent through longevity or wealth or position. The activities and institutions they reported on were those that the "core" population felt were important to the ongoing life of the town or city. From the later perspective of academic historians, this was elitist history: history of the successful, by the successful, for the successful.

These amateur local historians assiduously collected documentary and artifactual evidence and produced accounts of their communities that were little more than listings or excerpts from their evidence. Most were not talented writers, and their histories and gazetteers and atlases and guides and cyclopedias usually lacked any indication that they had even tried to construct a chronological, descriptive narrative. From the later vantage point of scholars, their accounts stand somewhere between compendia of raw evidence and actual writing.

During the early and mid-nineteenth century, amateur local historical writing was published locally by subscription, an indication that it was not a well-established genre of writing. By midcentury, however, such writings had become sufficiently popular for certain publishers—everywhere on the continent—to publish extensive lists of titles. Indeed, among the larger regional and national publishers, this type of historical writing became formulaic, the product of hired scribes who churned out historical and biographical sketches whose forms were laid down in editorial head-offices. By the twentieth century, well-known national publishing firms sometimes had well-established writers, who could tell a story well, produce local histories, usually of well-known towns or cities.

Through all of these developments, however, true amateurs flourished only in a few particular contexts. By the early nineteenth century, early New England towns, legatees of Puritan local community-building, contained many lovers of the past who saw the Puritan village as a very special place, one whose history was eminently worth preserving. Over the next century, a tradition of amateur local historical writing developed only in New England. Elsewhere, the most comprehensive histories were of cities and were produced by prominent individuals, often acting as editors for various contributors, who together sought to chronicle the emergence of those rare local communities that had become large-scale urban centers. Elsewhere, true amateurs were lone figures thinly scattered around a vast continent.

Amateur local historical writing in the United States achieved its mature form as a commercial venture. There were local elites everywhere who wanted to be associated with the life and reputation of their communities, but there weren't enough dedicated amateurs to produce the publications those elites would support. It is in this context that certain firms developed formulaic local history. The support of these local elites was contingent on their being given appropriate recognition in the various community-oriented publications.

Prominent persons became the subjects of biographical sketches and (some of them, at any rate) the subscribers of the histories of the early amateurs. By midcentury, support came in a somewhat different form. Locally prominent persons directly paid to have a biographical sketch placed in a local (whether town, city, or county) history. The association of prominent persons with community-focused publications became so popular that these paid-for sketches often became the largest section of the community's "history." Similarly, the town, city, and county atlases that were published in large numbers during the last third of the century (before the advent of areal photography) routinely contained paid-for sketches of the houses and firms of a given area's elite.

What had changed at midcentury was that these sketches and illustrations were not of historically prominent persons, as they had been in the early phases of amateur historical writings. Instant historical status and prominence was given to the living, at least to those willing and able to pay to be included in a given publication. Future generations would find particular individuals depicted as outstanding citizens at the time a book was published, not because their families had attained prominence over the course of a community's history. Thus, commercial considerations significantly influenced the way local history was published, as well as its form and content.

By the twentieth century—particularly during the 1920s, 1930s, and 1940s—national publishers detected that there was a substantial market for local history as another form of storytelling, a factual counterpart of fiction. Accordingly, they found accomplished writers to tell the story of the past of famous towns and cities, places that people everywhere already knew about. This rather short-lived genre of local historical writing was another indication of the importance of commerce in determining what forms local historical writing assumed.

By the depression of the 1930s, however, the vitality seemed to drain away from this great, sprawling enterprise in historical preservation. As life in North America and elsewhere in the modern world became progressively enlarged in scope and scale, individual lives became increasingly influenced by activities and institutions with a continental or even global dimension. Association with a given locality seemed to matter less and less. The very elite that had comprised a "core" population and had gained status from calling attention to their linkage to a particular town or city became increasingly mobile, less fixed in their residence over a lifetime. They became less concerned that their lives be recorded as a part of "their" community, past or present, and more concerned that they be identified with their occupation or profession, which was organized in ways that went far beyond a given locality. When a new elite—academic historians—took up the task of studying the past of local communities, beginning in the 1970s, they found local historical writing moribund as a genre of writing.

As already indicated, amateur historians, whether out of love or out of profit, did not have recognizably analytical, conceptual minds. For instance, no one ever commented on the discrepancy between dealing with a town or city as a political entity (with a particular territory and population and government) and a community defined socially (as only those inhabitants who were prominent or long established)—as the amateurs routinely did.

And yet, there was an embryonic sense of conceptualization, not something usually articulated, but something present here and there in their work. For example, a few of the historians of cities did comment on what factors resulted in their community's emergence as an urban center. All good amateurs dealt with many aspects of their community's life, all that they had evidence for, and this at a time when the emergent academic profession was narrowly focused on the nation conceived as a political entity. The amateurs had a broad definition of what community life consisted of. And even though their interest in the population was largely confined to the local elite, their biographical sketches are an early form of family history. Furthermore, their interest in atlases and illustrations of homes and buildings reveals an at least limited awareness of the physical dimensions of their communities.

Among academic scholars who have focused on community within the United States, sociologists especially, but also anthropologists, and, more recently, geographers, have long dominated the study of local settlement. Hence, historical study from local perspectives was ignored until historians themselves thought such settlements were worthy of examination on their own terms. So fixed on the national and, to some extent, regional perspectives were these academic historians that they largely ignored the local dimension of life in the history of the United States until the 1970s. Frederick Jackson Turner's plea in 1893 that a newly emerging profession focus on the frontier as the key to understanding American life greatly influenced colleagues to take account of the regional perspective in their work, even if the frontier itself was a movable region, but Turner's influence did not lead to a sudden awareness of the importance of local communities.[1] Similarly, Arthur Schlesinger's insistence in 1940 that cities had played as fundamental a role in the development of American life as the frontier did not result in a rush among his colleagues to study that past from an urban perspective.[2]

Not until these academic historians, whose "field" had always been defined in national terms, understood that, before the twentieth century, the lives of those they had been studying in their guise as "Americans" had actually been more influenced by their local communities than by their nation, could there be a sufficient shift in consciousness for significant numbers of these scholars to study rural neighborhoods and towns and cities from their own perspectives. As I argue in *Families and Communities* (1974), a "critical mass" of historians had reached this awareness by 1970, so that, henceforth, scholarly inquiry within the field of U.S. history would very likely be multiperspectival.

It is easy to demonstrate that, starting significantly in the 1970s, academic historians of the United States became increasingly aware of the kind of inquiries that their scholarly brethren in the social sciences had been making since the early twentieth century. In essence, they have found that the sociologists who dominated this study in its earlier phases—at least through the 1960s, concentrated on the processes of urbanization and of rural life and were not especially concerned with the nature of urban and rural communities, of towns and cities. Unquestionably, social scientists, particularly sociologists, have been far more concerned to define these processes rather than the actual communities that exist within rural and urban areas. This has been the case in both subfields that sociology divided into: rural and urban.

Like academic scholars and scientists of all descriptions, both of these groups of sociologists have chosen particular contexts to find evidence of general phenomena. Urban sociologists have always tried to work within theoretical frameworks in their quest for answers to the following question: Why have particular local communities undergone a process of what Eric Lampard has called "population concentration resulting in the formation of cities."[3] Urban sociology has been a respectable subspecialty of the discipline since the 1920s, and so academic historians have had a literature of considerable richness and variety to pick over.[4] By the 1960s, journal articles written by historians such as Eric Lampard[5] and Roy Lubove[6] summarized for their colleagues how urban sociologists had been organizing their study of the urbanization process.

By contrast, from the 1920s through the 1950s, rural sociologists heavily depended for their studies of rural life on funding from the U.S. Department of Agriculture routed through various governmental agencies. At least one critic was led to charge that this group's findings lacked a truly scholarly independence and perspective.[7] Whether or not such scholars have mirrored their sponsors' or clients' ideology and have been unable to experience rural communities from any point of view incompatible with that of the inhabitants of those communities, rural sociologists have nonetheless produced a great outpouring of studies of particular aspects of rural life.[8] What they have failed to produce, however, is theoretical constructs that have animated their work in the way that the urban sociologists have. As a result, sociological writings on rural life have been more notably descriptive than analytical or theoretical.[9] It is revealing that, beginning in the 1970s, when several academic historians presented general "state of the literature" articles on rural society they largely ignored the earlier work of rural sociologists. Instead, they referred to the approaches developed by historians themselves in the United States and elsewhere.[10]

In their collective effort to understand both rural and urban society, sociologists, and more recently, anthropologists and geographers have not been especially concerned to define actual local communities by size, as, say, hamlets or villages or towns or cities, preferring instead to situate all such communities along a continuum, from rural to urban. Social scientists have been far more focused on finding an overall definition of a community than in defining what sort of a local community they happen to be studying. With the exception of anthropologists, who have worked with the concept of levels of community for many decades,[11] the prevailing assumption has been that whatever community is, it is local and not national in scale.[12] The very political entities that have defined fields of study for historians have not attracted the attention of most groups of their social science brethren as a form of community. To the extent that sociologists, for example, have devised a categorization for nations it has been that they are a form of society.

The social scientists' search for a definition of community has turned, as do all scholarly quests for definition, into a ceaseless quest for an ever-elusive consensus. In 1955, sociologist George A. Hillery Jr. decided to survey the various efforts of social scientists to define community. He found no fewer then ninety-four different definitions in the scholarship he examined! The definers used as many as sixteen different concepts in their effort to find a meaning for the term. Hillery concluded, however, that most scholars were "in basic agreement that community consists of persons in social interaction within a geographic area and having one or more additional common ties."[13]

In the years that followed, other sociologists added to this massive effort. In 1959, Harold Kaufman sketched an "interactional" model that emphasized the interaction of three elements: the actors or participants (or community dwellers), the various groups they belonged to, and stages or phases of change (that a community passes through).[14] In the same year, Albert J. Reiss, Jr., defined community as a territorial system, that is, a sharing of space for residence, for sustenance, and for social functions involving common needs.[15] A year later, in 1960, Willis A. Sutton, Jr., and Jiri Kolaja defined community as human social interaction involving a number of families residing in a relatively small area, having developed a sociocultural system with which they identify and through which they solve problems.[16] By the 1960s, sociologists who tried to define community, instead of relying wholly on their own efforts, summarized definitions that seemed most persuasive to them. This was the case with Roland L. Warren in his well-known sociological text entitled *The Community in America* (1963)[17] and with Richard L. Simpson, in "Sociology of the Community: Current Status and Prospects" (1965).[18]

During these same years, largely unknown to sociologists, several anthropologists were also trying to define community from the perspective of their own discipline. In 1956, Robert Redfield, though interested primarily in studying primitive, small, local communities, insisted that a community—of whatever dimension and scale—be regarded as "a human whole[,] an integral entity describable on its own characteristics as a whole."[19] In the same year, Conrad M. Arensberg argued that there are variable, comparative terms that apply to all human and animal communities: (1) individuals (who?), (2) spaces (where?), (3) times (when?), (4) functions (what?), and (5) structure and process.[20] In 1961, Arensberg added that a community is territorially defined, with an ecology, that is, a resource base, but also an ongoing human habitat, and both spatial and temporal in nature, but also populational and generational.[21]

This sampling of the ongoing efforts of sociologists and anthropologists to define community during the 1950s and 1960s is sufficient to indicate that the historians who, by the 1970s, turned their attention to the study of local communities could have drawn on a conceptual framework for what they were probing. But the new academic local historians have generally remained unaware of these attempts to provide an overall definition for all local communities. Instead, urban historians have followed the lead of the urban sociologists and focused on the processes involved in urbanization, while historians of towns and rural neighborhoods have ignored the writings of rural sociologists and tried by their own devices to devize a new subfield of historical study.

7

A Historical Definition of Local Communities

It has been proper for academic local historians to ignore the efforts made by social scientists to provide an overall definition of community because social scientists have been largely unaware of the shifting character of community itself over time and space, through human history. Thus, they have reduced the variety and flux and complexity of the way humans have organized themselves in communities in the past. Social scientific definitions of community have generally been too schematic, too fixed or inflexible, too oriented toward the present. At the same time, academic historians of urban life (though not historians of towns) have concentrated too heavily on "process" and not enough on actual communities, which I would like to define from a historical perspective.

It seems to me that what limits the social scientists' efforts to define community is that, however insightful (and I believe that the attempts I have just referred to are all credible efforts to probe to the essence of what characterizes human communities), their authors have all lacked a recognition that a given community actually changes shape and form and size, depending on what aspect a scholar is investigating. Communities can be likened to amoebas that change their shape before our eyes as we poke and probe them. Thus, those who have lived in communities belong to or identify with entities with a profoundly protean character. The ordinary "inhabitants" of such communities have always had to live with a recognition of this obvious, but largely unarticulated, fact. The immediate context of their lives has always assumed varying shapes, depending on whether they have acted in a political, economic, social, cultural-intellectual, or ecological manner.

I would like to illustrate this way of defining community by referring to two communities that meant the most to me in my formative years, one small, the other large: Deerfield and Boston, Massachusetts.

*

Both Deerfield and Boston can be defined as political entities, with great precision, given that towns (or townships, to give Deerfield its proper political terminology) and cities have precisely demarcated territories, with exact geographic boundaries. Such local communities have been founded as "permanent" entities with fixed borders (unless altered by a specific political act). This is in sharp contrast to the seasonal villages of the "settled," agriculturally oriented tribes that white settlers came into contact with in various parts of the continent. In this sense, towns and cities have shared with states (or provinces) and nations and empires the characteristic of having ongoing, definite territorial shapes. This quality has given these political entities an unusually fixed nature, in notable contrast to the flux and indeterminancy so basic to the shape of the other dimensions of life.

In the case of both towns like Deerfield and cities like Boston, governments govern these territories. But what different meanings these political arrangements have! Deerfield, as a politically defined "township," is far larger than the particular settlements within it. There are "sections" of Deerfield whose inhabitants perceive "their" place as being in some senses as different from all the others—names such as Wapping, the Bars, East Deerfield, West Deerfield, South Deerfield, "Old" Deerfield (the original settlement). From the perspective of the individual inhabitant of Deerfield, government deals with a greater entity than his or her "place" and can seem larger than it should be. Deerfieldites are most aware of their political community when they are participating in the political process: voting for officers, petitioning, protesting, attending town meetings where the entire citizenry votes on matters to be decided by the town. So, community awareness waxes and wanes, depending on the time of year and the presence of matters suitable for political action.

In the case of Boston, government seems far smaller than the community. The city lines, the territory over which Boston's local government presides, take in a fraction of what Boston as a metropolis covers. In many aspects of local life, Boston as an urban area comprises a geographic entity far larger than the "city" of Boston defined politically. Many political matters are dealt with by jerry-built, special governmental agencies that have jurisdiction for particular purposes over varying amounts of politically defined suburbs as well as the central city. In many senses "Boston" is perceived by the several million inhabitants who live in the Boston area as an urban community divided into a thatchwork of political jurisdictions. Many matters of general concern are dealt with by appointed, supralocal agencies with only an indirect connection to a citizenry, who, divided into many "cities," elect representatives (councilors or aldermen or selectmen) whose jurisdiction is quite limited and partial both territorially and substantively. Yet, awareness of one's "political" community is still linked to actual local government: one's political community is still Somerville or Watertown or Chelsea, not metropolitan Boston.

Deerfield and Boston are typical of the thousands of towns and the hundreds of cities in the United States, however those towns and cities are defined politically, in the sense that all local communities cannot by their very nature have a political existence that is of precisely the same shape as the other aspects of community life.

Deerfield's and Boston's governmental systems are the result of conscious decisions taken centuries ago by the population of an entire region who created a uniform local political system. Deerfield and Boston as political entities were created out of a shared conviction that the political system for local communities should be of a certain character—comprised of townships—for all who inhabited such communities in Massachusetts, Rhode Island, Connecticut, Maine, New Hampshire, and Vermont. The long-term unwillingness of that population to change the basic character of this system has produced the discrepancies just noted.

The populations of other colonies and, later, states copied some aspects of the way New Englanders organized their towns and cities politically. The people of New York, Pennsylvania, Ohio, Illinois, Wisconsin, Minnesota, Missouri, and Arkansas all made incorporated townships coterminus with the entire territory of the state, as New Englanders had, although all gave greater power to county-level government than was the case back East. The people of all other states left unincorporated territory directly under the jurisdiction of county government. In many states, towns and cities and boroughs were directly incorporated within unincorporated county territory.[1]

Without question, local government, whether exercised primarily at the municipal or the county level, was the most important level of government throughout the vast territory of what became, after 1787, the United States of America. This was the case at least until the twentieth century, when the state and federal levels of government used their tax and regulatory authority to progressively augment their authority. The primacy of local government was established at a time when life was organized primarily in localized contexts. Later, as developments in communication and transportation made possible enlargements in the scale of the way life was organized, political authority was shifted upward and was assumed by the state and then federal levels of government.

The prevailing ideas and practices that resulted in the creation of legally and politically defined local communities were held as a legacy of their European origins by the white Europeans settlers and their progeny throughout the vast North American continent. "Americans" collectively believed that local government ought to be democratic or at least representative, regulating but generally not owning or directly managing the economic, social, or cultural life of the people.

Since the early seventeenth century, however, the range of authority and of activity of local government (and of all other levels of government) has been significantly augmented. More specifically, there has been a movement away from privately owned facilities (docks, bridges, turnpikes, wells, privies) to public utilities (public streets, municipal sewer and water systems); from private power sources (wind, water, steam) to public/private mixes of energy supply (publicly owned electrical firms alongside privately owned); from volunteer agencies (fire companies, charitable groups) to professional departments of municipal governments (police and fire) or to mixed, public/private institutions (hospitals).

Shared beliefs made possible the creation and maintenance of a multitude of similarly conceived local municipalities, which were given the most important tasks of governance until the twentieth century. In this way, localized, largely isolated, politically defined communities embraced the lives of most of the inhabitants of North America until our century but were of the same character throughout the continent.

As urbanized communities have grown, they have added territory, just as the nation has, through annexation. This has been the case throughout the continent until such time as suburbanites have balked and have refused to be politically amalgamated to an expansionist urban center, seeking instead to retain at least a political definition for their community that is limited, contained, town-like, even rural. By contrast, townships and counties have tended to evolve, not by annexation, but by secession, by splitting up into progressively greater numbers of communities covering increasingly smaller amounts of territory. Through all these developments, states, though they grew steadily in number until the early twentieth century, once admitted to the union by Congress, have, virtually without exception, retained their original political boundaries. In this sense, they have been the most unchanging political entities in the American federal system.

It was state (and before it, colonial) government that assumed responsibility for the legal creation, through incorporation and the granting of charters, of local communities. States have also created various forms of town and city government and have fixed the varied population levels that a town has to reach in order for its government to apply for city status. Thus, the states have defined in a variety of ways what a town is and what a city is, at least in a political sense. On the federal level, the Census Bureau has also defined—by category and population levels—rural areas, rural places, and urban places. But this federal effort to give local communities a precise definition has, in reality, simply added another layer of definitions. The Census Bureau has not followed the various states' definitions and forms of incorporations. Instead, it has devised its own schemes for categorizing "places," with all places of more than 2,500 inhabitants having been designated as "urban" since 1890 and with the burgeoning metropolitan centers being more recently defined in various ways as their existence has become too obvious to ignore, even if the states continue to do so.

The people who have lived within the United States and its colonial predecessors have thus forged local communities of a political kind with a bewildering mixture of encrusted tradition and change or flux. The result has been the evolution of hundreds of cities and thousands of towns, like Boston and Deerfield, which have assumed a variety of political shapes and forms.

Some local communities have been established as special, wholly political communities. County seats and state capitals have often been chosen only after a fierce competition for the right to locate county or state political institutions in a given community. There have also been frontier garrisons and forts and, more recently, military bases—that is, specially created military-centered towns, dependent on the activity of the military services, which are governmental or political instrumentalities.

*

If towns such as Deerfield and cities such as Boston are perceived as physical entities, a rather stark contrast is evident. In townships, though this is far less the case in tightly demarcated towns and boroughs, the human-built setting is scattered in villages sporadically located around the politically defined community. In the purely physical sense, Old Deerfield, South Deerfield, West Deerfield, East Deerfield, the Bars, and Wapping are far smaller territorially than is the township of Deerfield. Towns defined in this physical sense are, from an air-borne perspective, a vast number of peculiarly shaped entities scattered through the continental landscape.

By contrast, if cities like Boston are viewed from above as physical shapes, the contiguous human-built settlement of an urban complex is vast and continuous, stretching over a large geographic area, extending far beyond the city limits of Boston itself. So extensive are the largest urban metropolises across the continent that the U.S. Census Bureau has raced to find names to keep up with the spatial reality of urban areas that increase their distance and size like fast-moving shadows.

As far as the actual layout of local communities is concerned, there have not been sharp distinctions between towns and cities. It is more revealing to examine local communities along a continuum or spectrum of various-sized communities. The spatial arrangements of smaller local communities have lacked the clarity and obviousness of those of larger local communities, but physically defined settlements—above the threshold of minimum-sized hamlets—have all tended to display spatial arrangements of a similar kind.

Typically during the seventeenth and eighteenth centuries, but with decreasing frequency during the nineteenth century, workplace and living space were shared quarters for farmers, craftsmen, and even professional people. During these years, residential and occupational or economic uses of the built structures in physically defined local communities typically overlaid one another, and both the smaller and the larger types of local communities lacked clearly demarcated districts with respect to use. But once residences and workplaces became separated, when industrial, commercial, and retail activity became large-scaled and involved the employment of distinctive workplaces—offices, factories, stores—both towns and cities tended to become divided into districts of either an economic or a residential character. This was especially the case with larger urban centers like Boston, where such communities were subdivided into residential districts based on wealth or income levels. In quite small local communities or towns like Deerfield, however, the same tendency to split physical settlements into districts based on residential or economic use is evident, though less engrained.

The district or districts used for economic purposes in human-built physical settlements have also tended to be located at the focal point of those settlements. In all local communities above the level of a hamlet, industrial/commercial/retail properties have typically had central locations, and residences have been situated around this center. Similarly, transportation and communication depots—whether livery stables for horses, gas stations for motor vehicles, railroad stations, bus stations, post offices, telephone exchanges, newspaper offices, or radio and television stations—have also tended to be located centrally within local communities of all sizes.

During the twentieth century, however, developments both in transportation and communication and in demographic patterns have decentralized the physical makeup of local communities. As urbanized areas of any dimension have, demographically, seeped or hemorrhaged outward and as modes of road and rail and air transport have steadily speeded the movements of people and their goods, the spatial arrangement of local communities has become significantly less centralized.

Highways bypass (as well as continue to go through) towns, just as interstates go around (as well as through) urban areas. Airports are only vaguely associated, in terms of their location, with the urban communities they serve. Even railroad and bus stations are sometimes relocated to the outskirts of a town or a city. Post offices, newspaper offices, and radio and television stations are sometimes displaced from their central locations. Industrial production facilities and retail centers have often been moved out from the centers toward the edges of communities. Even consolidated municipal offices, schools, and churches have on some occasions been relocated away from earlier central locations.

Decentralization has to some extent been accompanied by the reintegration of the workplace with the home, as telecommunications make possible an increasing number of home-based occupations. Thus, local communities have at least partially returned to a preindustrial melding of home and work in their spatial arrangements.

In another dimension of towns and cities as physical settlements, the particular styles (or appearances) of each of the human-made products used by the inhabitants—their "material culture"—have had their own "cultural areas," each different in shape and size and territory from all the others. House styles; designs for various forms of furniture and other household furnishings; clothing fashions; food and drink recipes; layouts of farm, craft, industrial, commercial, and retail buildings; shapes of consumer products of various kinds—all extend territorially beyond individual settlements in varying shapes, some as wide as European civilization itself, and others as narrow as a particular township and its environs, but all linking the inhabitants of particular settlements to a wider context, obviously different in size and shape from their politically defined territories. For example, there are, in Deerfield, Connecticut Valley doorways and, sold over vast areas, Boston rockers.

During the twentieth century, however, as developments in communication and transportation have made possible a much larger scale of organization, many of these regional and local stylistic variations have given way to an increasing uniformity over wider and wider areas. Domestic and commercial architecture, clothing, furniture and appliances, motor vehicles—all have been shaped by corporate designers whose styles have become continental and global in scope, producing what Daniel J. Boorstin has called the "everywhere community."[2]

*

Towns such as Deerfield and cities such as Boston, as ecological/geographical entities, consist of all the land and water—the entire topography—encased within the precise, politically defined boundaries or borders of each: all the ponds and lakes and brooks and rivers and shores and marshes and swamps and forests and mountains and hills and valleys and plains. Those who have provided cartographical depictions (maps) of local communities, and states and nations as well, have often overlain geographical and political territories: topographical lines and political boundaries are presented together. In no other context does the fixity of politically defined territory and community grate more against the natural flow of human activity than in this juxtaposition of the ecological and the political.

Since political boundaries of any kind have rarely followed natural geographic contours, local communities—again, like states and nations—have usually lacked a meaningful ecological/geographical definition, and it has been difficult for their populations (if defined politically, economically, or socially) to perceive of themselves as a community for purposes of relating to the land and water and air around them. For example, there are Deerfield meadows and farm fields, ponds and river-bottom lands, but the Deerfield River doesn't stop at Deerfield's political borders any more than the Deerfield Valley does. One shore of the Charles River forms some of Boston's city limits, but the Charles River basin is shared with many other politically defined communities. (Similarly, New York and Pennsylvania, as states, share the Appalachian Mountains, just as the United States and Canada share the Rocky Mountains.) So, although towns and cities (and states and nations) contain political borders that enclose some geographical features, there are many others that go beyond those borders.

Of course, any human community depends for its survival on its ecological/geographical setting. The economic and recreational lives of townspeople like Deerfieldites and city inhabitants like Bostonians have been inextricably linked to their ecological/geographical setting, but that setting has varied in size, depending on the nature of the activity, sometimes confined within their political boundaries, sometimes extending beyond them. For example, tobacco farms used to be situated throughout the appropriate ecological setting of the Connecticut River Valley. Their range and location had little to do with Deerfield as a community.

The vast amounts of public land that both the federal and state governments offered for sale during much of the eighteenth and nineteenth centuries were surveyed on the basis of rectangular lots, having little to do with the natural contours of the landscape—an orderly, rational system, but economically myopic. "Squatters" (those who settled on and improved public land without legal entitlement) understood how ill-fitting these legally defined land boundaries were and occupied parcels of land that at least made economic sense to them.[3] As for politically defined local communities, state and local politicians have rarely established towns, townships, boroughs, or cities whose borders or boundaries fit into geographically cohesive areas. The result has been that when people have encountered problems relating to the use of their ecological or geographical setting, they have rarely had well-situated levels of government to deal with those problems.

When towns and cities are examined within regional geographic settings, however, then the shaping force of the environment can be seen much more clearly. The geographic patterns of New England, the mid-Atlantic, the South, the Midwest, the Plains, the Rocky Mountains, and the Pacific Coast all provide a meaningful perspective from which to explore the effects of geography—of water and soil and climate—on all the dimensions of town and city life, but most importantly on the economic one.

The relative presence or absence of soil suitable for agriculture was a fundamental factor in determining the incidence of farming in all areas of the continent—little in New England, more in the mid-Atlantic, still more in the South, yet more in the Midwest, less in the Plains, and rich pockets in the Pacific Coast—just as the presence of forests or minerals or coastal fishing banks determined where extractive activity developed. Similarly, the presence of harbors along coasts and geographically defined inland "breaks" in transportation provided the settings where urban centers could grow, and water"falls" were the sites for milling and early industrial activity.

In the twentieth century, geography, though still a significant factor in shaping towns and cities, has become somewhat less vital in that electricity is a power source that allows industrial activity to be located virtually anywhere, just as developments in telecommunications permit commerce to be carried on outside urban centers.

*

What are Deerfield and Boston when defined as economic entities? What shape do they assume when examined from an economic standpoint? One way to determine this aspect of local community life is to ask what territory those who resided in Deerfield and Boston, defined as political entities, covered in the course of their economic activities. Another way is to query what space firms of various sizes located within the township or the city operated on. In either case, the actual physical space that persons or firms occupy when engaging in economic activity differs from that of the politically defined town or city in spatial or territorial terms.

Most local communities have been founded and settled for economic purposes. They are what Page Smith has called "cumulative," that is, sustained, enlarged, or diminished because of economic activity.[4] With few exceptions, the economic activity generated by the inhabitants of a politically defined community has been the most significant determinant of a local community's size, of that community's history of growth, stability, or decline. There have also been special local communities founded with a clearly planned economic purpose: the early mill villages of water-powered machine production; the company towns, wholly built by firms in order to attract wage laborers to new forms of industry or to remote locations near mines and forests; railroad towns, developed by firms connected to railroad corporations who thereby induced settlement along economically marginal rights of way.

Local communities (defined as physical, built-up settlements), of whatever size, have usually been service centers for an outlying population of a greater size and territory than the community itself. The larger the community, the greater the array of services it has provided, and the larger the area it has served.

Whenever the inhabitants of politically defined towns and cities have performed particular economic functions for larger populations, then, for those people, their "local community," defined economically, has expanded to embrace that larger territory, which for economic purposes becomes part of the given town or city. By contrast, other inhabitants of politically defined local communities may engage in economic activity that involves only a portion of that community. In either case, the actual spatial shape produced by economic activity differs from that of the politically defined territory. The most obvious example of this is that the planned communities with an economic purpose—mill villages, company towns—often bore little relationship to politically defined town(ship)s.

When Deerfield, like other hamlets, villages, or towns, served as a service center for farmers, then the agricultural area surrounding it became part of Deerfield as an economic entity. Similarly, when milling or craft activities involved people from the adjoining rural areas, then Deerfield was enlarged thereby. Horse and, later, motor vehicular transportation determined the extent of this area: individuals and groups in the countryside decided which easily reached nearby town had the services they wanted. And, when early, water-powered machine production in factories appeared in various towns (though not Deerfield), railroad transport greatly extended the ambit of the economic activity of a particular small, local community. Such products were the result of an admixture of material, labor, financing, marketing, and consumption that involved people over large territories. In recent decades, when electrically powered industry moved to the outskirts of Deerfield and other towns, it similarly drew on a mixture of elements from a wider area, including laborers and managers who commute in vehicles, just as in urban communities.

Throughout all of these economic developments, Deerfieldites have been aware that they have dealt in their economic activities with an enlarged or diminished but always different territory or space than that of their political township.

Urban centers like Boston are those rare local communities that have burgeoned into centers of commerce and, more recently, industry as well as of transportation and communication because of favorable locations and the entrepreneurial skills of their business people. Boston and other cities take on an enlarged economic aspect as towns like Deerfield have, though on much larger scale. Boston's craft or, later, electrically powered factory production has had an immense reach through its metropolitan rail and, more recently, air freight terminals and systems which have had a regional and then national reach. The goods and services of this large urban area have been advertised in newspapers and, more recently, on radio and television, of metropolitan scope (and beyond). The central city and, more recently, the suburbs themselves in a criss-cross pattern, employ people who have lived in a progressively larger commuter "catch-basin," whose size has been determined by evolving forms of transportation—foot, horse, trolley, motor vehicle, bus, subway, airplane. As a center of communications and transportation, Boston has provided a great array of economic and social services for an entire region.

Not all economic activity in Boston and environs took on this enlarged character: some was truly local, involving particular neighborhoods or particular suburbs only. But many individuals and firms have operated out of the Boston urban area and have in fact occupied an enlarged world when operating in an economic capacity. If living in Boston as defined politically, or even in its contiguously settled suburbs, these individuals and firms have augmented the "Boston" community in an economic sense. In either case, the economic community of Bostonians, either at the level of the individual or the firm, has been different from the space occupied by Boston as a political community.

It is difficult to define towns and cities as different economic entities in ways that remain true over long periods of time. Because all local communities are in some sense service centers for larger populations, it is more insightful to think, as geographers have, of a continuum of communities, with each community offering a range or scale of services linked to size. Even cities have sometimes been service centers for rural people and, with electrical power, the site for machine production, thus assuming economic functions originally connected with towns. With the enlargement in the scale of economic activity that has so marked the twentieth century, firms of all kinds that are continental or even global in scope have established and sustained branch plants and branch offices or franchised outlets in local communities of varying sizes, which means that truly local firms and these "nonlocal" ones directly compete in many communities.

The economic activity associated with towns like Deerfield and cities like Boston has been similar throughout the North American continent, wherever labor, materials, investment capital, entrepreneurial and managerial skill, and markets have existed in tandem. Just as the European settlers and their descendants have shared common political ideals for the creation of politically defined local communities, so too have they shared a capitalist orientation economically. That is, they have favored private ownership and the accumulation of wealth as the chief goal of economic activity, favoring as well the material comfort and social status and political independence that are believed to be its direct consequences.

As a result, even though economic activity was typically limited to local and regional dimensions until the late nineteenth century, what people did economically in and around the great numbers of hamlets, villages, towns, and cities across North America has had a remarkable uniformity. This uniformity has only become more evident as the evolution of transportation and communication has made possible activity of continental and then even global dimensions. All the while, the shape or territory of local communities perceived as economic entities has rarely coincided with the political boundaries of such communities. In the same way, the spatial dimension of economic activities of a wider scale, activities involving firms or corporations of a regional, continental, or global scope, have rarely coincided with state or national political boundaries.

Governments at all levels of the federal political system have, of course, regulated and kept statistics on economic life, and it is routine for politicians at all levels to refer to "our" economy, as if the economy's shape coincided with the political community's: "America's" or the nation's economy, "Massachusetts'" or the state's economy, "Boston's" or the city's economy, "Deerfield's" or the town's economy. In this way, politicians try to extend the political community's definition to embrace the economic life of those who inhabit various levels of political communities. But this blurring of definitions does not change the fact that local communities always assume different shapes, depending on which aspect of life one is participating in or examining.

*

Deerfield and Boston as a town and a city, respectively, are also social entities each of which has its own dimensions, all differing in some sense from their political and economic shapes.

Massive geographic and social mobility has profoundly affected the stability and continuity of life in the local communities of North America. What has given towns and cities like Deerfield and Boston a measure of both stability and continuity has been the existence of a core population—that is, individuals and families who have lived on in the community across several generations. This element within the total populations (defined politically) has commonly believed that only they are true Deerfieldites or true Bostonians, while relative newcomers or immigrants, even though they too inhabit the territory of the politically defined community, are foreigners, "others," aliens.

Thus, in the perception of those who have spent a lifetime in Deerfield and Boston, the community defined socially has been significantly narrower than the political community. This excision of a sizable portion of the population is partly "interior," that is, a mental perception, an exclusion of certain groups from genuine membership in the social community. It is also partly a matter of physical, spatial segregation, as the "foreign" element often has wanted or has been forced to live in particular sections or neighborhoods of the town or city. For instance, Deerfield had the sections "Cheapside" and "Pigsville." In Boston, there were sections such as South Boston (Irish), the North End (Italian), and Roxbury (blacks). Some of the descendants of "newcomers" have stayed, thus establishing new elements in the core population. These groups are no longer regarded as outsiders, as genuine immigrants are, but there continues to be a widely shared sense that the truest inhabitants of Deerfield and Boston are those whose families have been there the longest. Such families continue to contribute prominent individuals to the community. But the much-increased mobility of the professional/managerial groups that, since the nineteenth century, has accompanied the enlarged scale of the way life is organized has to a considerable extent undermined the continuity and stability of a core population in towns and cities like Deerfield and Boston.

In another kind of social context, towns and cities have contrasted rather sharply, although there have also been special kinds of towns whose inhabitants have behaved in a "city-like" manner. Here I'm referring to the place of class in local community life. The white inhabitants of North America have drawn on notions of class derived from their European origins. However, from the beginning of white settlement, class has been more closely linked to levels of wealth in North America than in Europe. North American whites lacked inherited status as a basis for class when the European nobility failed to re-create itself across the Atlantic. However, the white settlers did create an inherited status for blacks through the institution of slavery.

As a general proposition, small local communities, or towns as social entities, have been dominated by their middle class: most inhabitants have been neither spectacularly rich nor abysmally poor. This social profile has meant that it has been easier for town dwellers to behave in a middle-class way. The relatively few poor or rich people have not had much influence in determining what constitutes a normal pattern of life in the community, the physically built-up portions of towns like Deerfield.

The composition of the middle-class inhabitants of towns has evolved, however. When the typical town was a service center for farmers, the profile consisted of those providing craft, milling, retailing, and professional services. Since the "free fall" in the number of those engaged in agriculture—from over 90 percent in 1790 to 2–3 percent in 1990—has significantly reduced the role of smaller local communities as centers for rural populations, the composition of the middle-class in towns has shifted. It now includes an influx of retired farmers from outlying areas, people who have returned to retire in their hometowns, ex-urbanites who have moved out of the cities because of urban problems, and "back-to-the-landers"/counterculturalists who have sought rural havens.[5]

A major consequence of the middle-class orientation of small, local communities has been the intolerance town dwellers have usually displayed toward those who fail to abide by the norms of middle-class behavior. Until recently, acceptable behavior has been rather clearly demarcated. Those who have not abided by these norms and who have behaved differently have experienced varying degrees of ostracism and criticism. Thus, inhabitants of rural communities have been socially conservative and have strongly supported crusades to end such forms of misbehavior as inebriation, gambling, and prostitution.

In contrast to towns such as Deerfield, cities such as Boston typically have deeply defined classes and exhibit a great gulf between the richest and poorest inhabitants. This class consciousness has been kept alive by the coexistence in the political community of large groups of rich, middle-class, and poor people, often segregated into particular neighborhoods geographically, physically, and spatially. Cities are socially divisive communities, and, in contrast to towns, the norms of behavior are less settled, more contested, or uncertain, with contrasting patterns in evidence for each of the major class groupings and with varying degrees of community tolerance for particular kinds of misbehavior.

But this is somewhat too schematic, and the reality of life in the continent's hundreds of cities and thousands of towns has been more complicated. Certain kinds of towns have displayed, even though quite small, the class cleavages usually associated with cities. Whenever townspeople have had access to a resource that an entrepreneurial group has known how to profit from, such communities have displayed the steeply vertical class profile of the cities. I'm referring here to towns located in or near large-scale industrial or forestry or mining or fishing or livestock or farming enterprises, such as the owner lived-in mill villages or the cattle towns.

Furthermore, as the scale of life has grown larger during the twentieth century, and as developments in communication and transportation have broken down the relative isolation that characterized local communities of all kinds, townspeople have become very influenced by city living. Specifically, they have increasingly derived their sense of class and standards of behavior from city dwellers. It has been increasingly difficult to distinguish town from city with respect to notions of class, to what constitutes upper, middle, and lower income, status, and proper behavior. Moreover, the recent influx of ex-urbanites, commuters, and counterculturists into many towns has reduced the socially conservative composition of middle-class town dwellers in many instances. So, what used to be an at least partially accurate basis for defining small and large local communities in a social context has become far less so during the twentieth century.

In yet another social definition for local communities, a sharp division has arisen between small and large communities. This division has remained the most important basis for demarcating towns from cities, and is more lasting and significant than any of the efforts by state and federal governments to legally distinguish small and large local communities politically on the basis of levels of population. I am referring to a mental perception of town dwellers and city inhabitants: the widely held view that, in a true town, life is lived in a personal way, that is, one knows and is known by everyone in the community) and that, in a real city, life is lived—beyond a small circle of people whom one knows well—impersonally, among passing strangers and among people with whom one has many different types of formal relationships. This particular social definition of local communities is based on physically defined settlements, but it defies statistical measurement because it is a mental perception.

In the case of Old Deerfield as a settled village, there is the sense (which I can personally vouch for) that indeed everyone does know and care about everyone else, or at least has heard or seen or touched or smelled everyone else. By contrast, in the sprawling urban complex called Boston, personal involvement is overwhelmed by movement among strangers or among those whom one relates to in formalized ways.

Behavior in towns, so defined, is marked by its informality, its relaxation of well-defined and maintained rules and regulations. The character or personality of particular individuals and groups outweighs the automatic application of legalized and formalized ways of behaving in a social context. By contrast, in cities, the relative impersonality of life makes it easier for inhabitants or visitors to apply formal rules in their social interactions. Urbanites have developed a kind of civility that makes possible the coexistence of large numbers of people not known to each other in a personal way.

Once again, however, the familiarity and informality of town life have produced an intolerance for strangers, for those who are different and unknown. Friendliness or at least acceptance is reserved for those already known as a result of shared living in a small-scaled, physically defined community. By contrast, the formality and impersonality of city living has produced a greater degree of tolerance of the varied kinds of strangers that populate an urban community.

Other definitions of local communities as social entities have also reflected significant differences between towns and cities. The inhabitants of local communities of all descriptions participate in leisure-time and recreational activities and join organizations (outside of their work life) such as churches; men's and women's and children's clubs; farmers' and laborers' and businessmen's clubs; service organizations; benevolent or reform groups; recreational clubs and sporting activity; arts and entertainment groups; and intellectual clubs. What has been distinctive about towns, defined as physical settlements, is that such groups have been communitywide. For example, in Old Deerfield the Men's and Women's Clubs were open to everyone in the village. There have also been specially created "resort" and "retirement" villages, designed solely to provide recreational services for everyone in the community, whether on vacation or in retirement. In cities, a social organization or activity has usually drawn on those living in particular neighborhoods or sections of the urban area.

This distinction between towns and cities has been significant because, in towns, these social activities have related to community in a way that has been impossible in larger, urban local communities. In towns, such social activities as visiting, playing sports or games, indulging in pastimes, and belonging to a club have signified that an individual still relates to the whole community, on the selective basis of a shared interest, to be sure, and in a rather informal, unstructured way. In cities, such associations have been more formalized and, although one has extended in a very limited way one's involvement with others, again on the basis of a common interest, the urban community has still been a place filled with strangers.

This particular distinction has become less clear in the course of the twentieth century, however. As the scope of organized life has become greatly enlarged, townspeople have increasingly come to belong to clubs and to engage in social activities that are local chapters and versions of phenomena of much larger dimensions: national and international associations of many kinds of organizations; fraternal clubs, for instance. Hence, town dwellers have created patterns of associations that are focused outward, beyond the immediate community, just as city inhabitants have, thus reducing the community orientation of earlier times.

There are still indigenous or truly local organizations in both towns and cities, however, and (like one-of-a-kind local economic firms) such clubs have to compete with the local chapters of "outside" organizations for members.

Another way to define towns and cities in a social context is to focus on the activities of their community teams and clubs and on their celebrations, those special occasions that mark particular days during the year. In both towns and cities, the local or municipal government often organizes or supports private groups who sponsor such teams and clubs and events. This means that competitions and celebrations frequently are organized on the basis of the politically defined community: the borough, town, township, or city. In much the same way, state and federal governments sponsor teams and celebrations of a state or national character.

In this way, government at all levels of the political system tries to instill a sense of community in the inhabitants of their respective political units. Another source of support for community-based competition and celebration has been "booster" or community-minded newspaper, radio, and television managers. Sporting teams and clubs of various kinds compete with others, whether on a national, regional, state, county, or local level. In doing so, they represent politically defined communities, whether in Deerfield or Boston, Massachusetts, New England, the United States, the Western Hemisphere, or the world. Teams representing every "level" of community compete as surrogate representations of the real community.

Sponsored celebrations at the anniversary of the founding of towns like Deerfield or cities like Boston are communitywide (with a political definition) commemorations of their history. They represent a special time of celebration whose sole purpose is to instill in the participants a sense of identity with, loyalty to, and pride for their communities. In addition, there are holidays that punctuate the year—some global, many national, a few state or local in nature. Each of these annual celebrations has its own character: New Year's, Easter, Independence Day, Labor Day, Halloween, Thanksgiving, Christmas. What distinguishes a town like Deerfield from a city like Boston in this context is that town competitions and celebrations are communitywide, whereas in cities these phenomena are confined to the patchwork of political jurisdictions that make up an urban area. Competition and celebration are linked to the whole community in small places like Deerfield, and are special occasions that draw together everyone who cares to attend from all over the community. Within a community context, these commemorations and events provide a focus that takes town dwellers beyond the mundane world of work and serve as reminders that the politically defined community is worthy of being identified with. When such activities occur in an urban complex like Boston, they lack a satisfactory community context, with the exception of events that are given a metropolitanwide definition (such as the Boston Marathon).

Finally, local communities provide the social context for the life passages of individual inhabitants, the setting for birth, baptism, graduation, marriage, death. Again, true town dwellers, as in Deerfield, undergo these rites of passage in a communitywide context in the sense that everyone in town (defined as a physical settlement) either participates or knows or learns about the event. In cities like Boston, individuals also experience these events, but their experience is shared with a minuscule portion of the metropolitan population.

Notice that in many of the instances where I've examined towns and cities in particular social contexts, the actual physical shape of the community assumed that of the human-built setting, not that of the politically defined territory. In many ways, a local community defined socially takes in the contiguously settled area, not the territory administered by government (and, in the case of the "core" population's perception of who is "in" the community, even less than the physically occupied area). Politicians have tried to induce the inhabitants of politically defined townships, towns, and cities to think of "their" community in a political sense whenever there has been a competition with other towns and cities and whenever the politically defined community has celebrated its history. For most purposes, however, the local community as a social entity has not coincided with itself as a political entity.

*

Deerfield and Boston, as a town and a city, can also be perceived as cultural-intellectual entities and, as such, assume still other shapes and forms.

The values, beliefs, and ideals of both townspeople, such as Deerfieldites, and city dwellers, such as Bostonians, have been forged in two institutional settings that have, at least in a spatial sense, further subdivided all local communities, big or small: the churches and the schools. As formal school systems were established, whether in townships, towns, boroughs, or cities, politically defined communities all over the continent were divided into school districts. Children received formal instruction in institutions linked to neighborhoods, cut-down forms of local communities, districts that were sometimes used for other purposes as well. Churches were built in many locations both within and outside of particular towns or cities, providing religious services for members who lived within or around the community as a built settlement.

The only context in which a single church has dominated a whole community has been in the special religious, utopian communities founded by particular religious groups and restricted for as long as possible to those groups alone. The Puritans in colonial New England were the most successful of these utopian religionists, but during the nineteenth century many smaller-scaled efforts were made by other religious groups.

Yet, although schools and churches physically subdivided politically defined communities into districts and parishes, these same secular and spiritual conduits also served to unite local community dwellers in a mental sense. The value and belief system derived from Christianity and its modern variant, humanism, are coterminus with European civilization itself, even though, as an organization, the church has been much divided. From the eighteenth century onward, among the varied Christian denominations and sects, an initial and divisive doctrinal orientation increasingly gave way to a common emphasis on what constituted proper Christian living. This meant that the churches, though still much divided in a physical, spatial, and organizational sense, came to play a uniform cultural/intellectual role: to transmit to their communicants a Christian and, more recently, a more broadly humanistic view of life. Beginning in the nineteenth century, among the vast and varied number of schools, an initial organizational variety was gradually replaced by increasing uniformity in the manner and content of what was taught. This growing uniformity came as a result of the creation of teacher training institutes and formally designed statewide school systems.

Although schools and churches (even among those denominations with well-developed hierarchical structures) have remained intensely local institutions, both have been affected by pressures to consolidate that have been produced by communication and transportation developments. As a result, during the twentieth century, the "consolidated" school has become as common a phenomenon as the closed-out rural or village church. As locally oriented institutions, schools and churches have played a vital role in the transmission of the entire cultural/intellectual "memory" of a civilization across a vast continent. The sermon and the school book have been major "carriers" of that civilization's values, beliefs, skills, and knowledge.

These two institutions have shared this task with a third institution, which, in its earliest form, also had a major presence in local communities of all kinds: the media or journalism. Newspapers have been vital local institutions, and various forms of news and editorial commentary have constituted another conduit for the transmission of useful information and Christian and humanistic values, alongside sermons and school books. If churches and schools have subdivided communities in a physical sense, newspapers have enlarged them, creating "reading areas," that are usually considerably larger than the community defined either politically or spatially. During the twentieth century, aural and visual means of communicating news and values via radio and television have been added to the older form of print media. This has occurred as developments in communication have enlarged the scope and scale of life and made possible national and international media organizations that are as concerned about the conveyance of global and continental news and information as they are about developments on a local level.

The values, beliefs, skills, and information that churches, schools, and the media have conveyed to the inhabitants of local communities of all sizes throughout the continent exhibits a basic uniformity. But the inhabitants of towns and cities have differed somewhat in the way they have dealt with the resulting orthodoxy. Town dwellers have typically sought to uphold the orthodox value and belief system so generated. They have usually been less tolerant than city inhabitants have of dissent, of reformers who, bothered by the existence of discrepancies between commonly held ideals and social reality, have proposed to reform and improve life, whether through political or extralegal means. It is revealing that the reform movements that have been the most popular in small local communities have been the temperance, anti-saloon, purity, and anti-vice crusades, all of which sought to end activity that was un-Christian. Supporters of such movements were orthodox in temperament, in the sense that they tried to sustain the existing Christian way of life by ending these violations of it.

In contrast, reforms that have involved the enlargement of justice or equality to include hitherto excluded elements in the population have generally been supported most visibly in urban settings, where the large, varied populations have enabled toleration of dissent to be most in evidence. Furthermore, from their inception, cities have been intellectual and transportation/communication centers. As such, they have contained institutions of higher learning where varied and dissenting views as to what constitutes the best ideals and values have been most likely to appear. Boston, for example, is a renowned center for higher educational institutions. Cities have also had the means to disseminate information, skills, and ideas through the evolving technological means of transporting people and communicating knowledge.

And yet, these distinctions between small and large local communities can be overdrawn and made too schematic. For instance, colleges and universities have also been located in towns, and, in some instances, college or university campuses have so dominated local communities that such communities exist largely because of their presence; these are the so-called college towns. Other towns, such as Deerfield, are centers for various kinds of private schools.

It was also the case that the most radical of all reform movements—at the local level—occurred in specially created villages, not in cities. More radical by far than the Puritans' community-building ventures of colonial times, during the nineteenth century, various "utopian socialist" groups, both secular and religious, founded settlements of a communitarian nature. That is, property was owned in common by the whole community, which was dedicated to peace, love, and harmony rather than competition, hostility, and division. No other groups were so radical in how they planned to improve or perfect life on the continent. But these groups were insular, isolated: theirs was an exclusionary utopian experiment and they had no blueprint for anyone else. As the scale of life broadened, such socialist undertakings became national and political. By the late nineteenth century, national socialist parties continued to advocate fundamental reform.

As cultural entities, as settings for entertainment, recreational, and artistic activities of all kinds, it is once again easy to outline distinctions between small and large local communities, defined as physical, built-up settlements. Townspeople, like Deerfieldites, have been less open to unorthodox forms of such cultural activity than have city inhabitants, like Bostonians, and have wanted it to measure up to prevailing moral standards. Entertainers and artists have not usually flourished in small local community settings, where people have emphasized the practical and the useful. Athletes have been far more acceptable, in both towns and cities, because they embody physical strength and perform with professional skill what everyone can attempt to do recreationally, as leisure-time activity.

Entertainers and artists, especially the unorthodox among them, have most easily existed in urban settings, with their large and varied populations. In addition, cities have been cultural centers, the locations for museums, galleries, publishers and bookstores and large libraries, lecture and concert halls, opera and ballet houses, theatres, and organizations of artists of all kinds. By contrast, towns often built catch-all "opera houses" as their single venue for culture. It was in cities that artistic, entertainment, and recreational activities first became organized and formalized.

Once again, however, distinctions between towns and cities can be overdrawn. Beginning in the nineteenth century, there have been a number of artists' colonies in remote and small communities, In both towns and cities (in urban neighborhoods), purely local, amateur cultural groups have always existed. The professionalization of such activity, though it occurred first in cities, has meant that local and nonlocal groups have competed for the attendance of the inhabitants of all kinds of local communities. Beginning in the nineteenth century, traveling entertainment troupes and lone individual performers—circuses, theatrical groups, musicians, dancers, singers—appeared in towns and cities all over the continent. During the twentieth century, developments in communication have resulted in the aural (through radio) and the visual (through television and cinema) re-creation of entertainment and art, so that people living in local communities of all kinds can simultaneously witness such activity.

*

Finally, towns like Deerfield and cities like Boston are symbolic entities, occupying "interior space" in the minds of those who identify with them.

Inhabitants of such towns and cities as physical entities perceive them in ways that nations or regions or states can never be perceived. Such towns and cities have been depicted by cartographers on maps, photographers in photographs, artists in drawings and paintings—thus providing several ways for individual inhabitants to "see" their entire community. Deerfieldites and Bostonians can witness their town or city unaided, by their own sight, while approaching it or looking down from a high, central vantage point. In either case, the tallest structure defines the visual, physical dimensions of the community, whether that structure be a church, a town or city hall, or a commercial tower.[6] In Old Deerfield, this "roland"[7] is the tower on the oldest church; in Boston, the towers of two insurance companies—the Hancock and the Prudential—fulfill this same function, each sporting an observation deck.

Towns like Deerfield and cities like Boston are depicted in verbal ways by journalists and travelers who provide descriptive accounts of such communities or by writers of fiction and playwrights who use actual local communities as the settings for their stories and plays. Composers have composed songs about towns or cities. (Boston is the subject of several well-known songs; Deerfield, alas, appears not to have been so honored.) Poets have occasionally written poems about such places. And ordinary inhabitants have sometimes written memoirs or autobiographies about the communities they grew up in or have continued to reside in.

From time to time town dwellers and urbanites have also smelled or tasted or felt something that has reminded them specifically of their local community. These are far less common or trustworthy sensory means of evoking a feeling of identity with one's home community than are visual and verbal means.

Towns, though not cities, can be interpreted as extensions of the family. Page Smith has argued that, in their pioneer phase, towns are "father"-like entities: communities that have been founded and built through strenuous effort. Towns that survive pass into a later "mother"-like phase: a time of stability, when nurturing and cultivating an aesthetic and moral sense are primary. From the child's perspective, towns can be likened to wombs; they are settings that provide sons and daughters with a special, communitywide preparation for adult life. Towns as "hometowns" resonate with psychological significance for those who grew up in them.[8]

By contrast, inhabitants of cities are unable to feel that their community is family-like. Cities can be likened to menageries, beehives, rabbit-warrens: they teem with life of a varied character. In this context, cities as communities are the opposite of towns, which are characterized by the known and the familiar.

Just as nations are imagined communities that evoke the loyalty and identity of their citizens, so, too, do local communities elicit emotional, rational, and psychological responses from their inhabitants. In all of the above instances, towns or cities have been witnessed or depicted in ways that produce "localism"—feelings and thoughts and psychological states through which town and city dwellers gain a sense of identity with a particular local community. In similar ways, "nationalism" affects these same individuals in their guise as citizens of the United States. Townspeople and urbanites alike have reacted with a mixture of positive and negative feelings toward "their" local community, however defined, depicted, or witnessed: they have shown mixtures of admiration and disgust, pride and embarrassment, nostalgia and suppression, fondness and anxiety.

The "localism" defined here, though similar to nationalism in many respects, differs somewhat as well. A nation is a politically defined community with unchanging territory (unless expanded or contracted through political acts). Nationalism has fostered the belief among the citizens of a nation (such as the United States) that a nation's citizens are distinctive in all other ways as well, even though in reality they aren't. Nationalism thus conjures up a set territory—fixed borders that encase life in all its dimensions.

*

As argued here, local communities are of varying sizes and shapes, depending on which dimension of life is being examined. The protean character of towns and cities is so essential to their existence as communities that localism has in no way undermined it. Local communities have never been perceived by their inhabitants as simply political entities. And those who have identified with a particular town or city have accepted its changeable shape and size, even though they usually haven't reflected on that essential characteristic. What names do people give to the actual locations where they live: their address, their home? To what extent does the shape of their setting change as they work and as they play, as they avail themselves of various economic and social and cultural activities and services? Any inhabitant of a town or a city could respond to these queries.

I believe that my definition of "local community" is historically accurate, at least for the territory covered by the United States. The argument presented here is not one that can be understood only by those well versed in the academic mode of thinking. Ordinary inhabitants of towns and cities have always understood that their community changes shape, depending on what they are doing or thinking or feeling. All that I have done is to articulate and investigate in a systematic way what people have always known. Perhaps this is the most significant role academics can play for the society around them.

In any case, since academic historians have studied local communities, starting in the 1970s in significant numbers, they have usually avoided the overall definitions for "community" provided by various breeds of social scientists, and properly so, I would argue. Those definitions have been too general, too fixed, too inflexible, and they have lacked a sensitivity to what I'm calling the protean character of local communities. Future studies by academic local historians would benefit from an awareness of my historically grounded definition.

Urban historians should, however, pay more attention than they have in the past to the actual urban context of the cities they have focused on. They have tended to ransack all manner of local communities for evidences of "urbanization," instead of studying the multifaceted life of an actual urban community. Town historians have avoided this overconcentration on process rather than communities by focusing their studies on actual towns, whether as case studies or as types. They have ignored the practice of rural sociologists—that rural life and regions rather than particular communities in rural areas should be studied—and I think their work has benefited from this ignorance. By contrast, urban historians have followed the lead of urban sociologists, and, more recently, historical geographers and economists, and have erred in their preoccupation with urbanization.

The fact is that it has mattered to a considerable extent whether a local community has been small (a town) or large (a city). The smallness or largeness—terms with definitions always relative to time and place—of a particular community is one of that community's essential features.[9] It is also the case, as I have shown, that there have been no neat and unchanging distinctions, that for specific reasons some towns have been like cities, and that what distinguished towns from cities during the seventeenth, eighteenth, and nineteenth centuries has become less significant as the scale of life has enlarged during the twentieth century.

The work of academic local historians of all descriptions would be enhanced if the definition of community that I've outlined here were to be employed. Such historians should understand that local communities constituted the most important level of community until the twentieth century and are, therefore, the most fruitful type to study in any period before the twentieth century.

Those who will be engaged in the ongoing study of towns and cities also need to keep in mind the paradoxical situation that until recently has inhered in the local community-building efforts that have taken place throughout North America. Although these communities were relatively isolated and although life for most of their inhabitants was local in most of its dimensions, townspeople and city dwellers nevertheless shared a belief in the fundamental characteristics of European civilization. That is, they were in sufficient agreement as to what constituted proper values and behavior and activity that life as lived in hundreds of cities and thousands of towns strewn across a vast continent was strikingly similar. In short, such historians need to take account of isolation combined with duplication. Only then will the essential nature of this most important of human communities become as clear as it should be.

8

Current Definitions of Community

Towns like Deerfield and cities like Boston are place communities—that is, social entities that occupy space or territory through time, although they can be perceived mentally, through the "interior space" of their inhabitants' minds. Such place communities have been founded in all parts of the continent, though far more regularly and heavily in some areas than in others. Geography has largely determined the spatial layout of these thousands of settlements. From the beginning, what distinguished these local communities from those of the agriculturally oriented native tribes was that the white Europeans who settled in North America intended their "places" to be permanent, not seasonal or temporary.

New Englanders built villages wherever a largely hilly, somewhat resource-poor topography made it feasible to do so. Those in the Mid-Atlantic established many mill villages and a relatively few county seats/market towns, both of which pockmarked the broad river valleys of the Appalachian Mountains. Southerners favored crossroad villages, many of which became county seats, as well as some fall-line mill villages along the tidewater and piedmont regions of the wide Southern coastal plains. Midwesterners, in the most sustained local community-building frenzy of all, founded service-center villages at regular intervals across the vast river basins of the central third of the continent. But in the semiarid plains and in the Rocky Mountains and the Pacific Coast mountains and valleys, settlement was quite sporadic, limited by a varied topography to resource-rich areas. All over the continent, villages grew into cities at locations where there were good harbors or, in the interior, natural "breaks" in transportation lines of whatever kind.

From the outset of the European settlement of North America and continuing until the end of the nineteenth century, there was also a significant and large rural population that lived outside of local communities defined as physically builtup settlements. Many of those who crossed the Atlantic and many of their progeny lived directly on farmsteads, and not in a recognizable local community of any kind. In the first federal census, taken in 1790, over 90 percent of the population with an occupation were listed as engaged in farming. This percentage had declined to 42.5 percent by 1880[1] and had fallen precipitously to a mere 2 to 3 percent by 1990. But throughout these centuries, most farmers in all parts of the continent have continued to live outside of local settlements.

During the twentieth century, the truly rural population has declined along with the enormous fall in the number of farmers, and there has been a clear movement throughout the continent toward more settled areas. So, although a significant geographically defined element of the U.S. population lived outside of local settlements during the seventeenth, eighteenth, and nineteenth centuries, this has been decreasingly the case during the twentieth century.

There has also been a high level of geographic mobility among the European, Afro-American (once slavery was ended), Asian, and Latin American migrants to the North American continent and among their descendants. This form of mobility, though it has varied from time to time and from place to place, has been a continuous and notable feature of life in modern North America. This has been so much the case that large and significant elements in the populations of towns and cities from coast to coast have been transient; that is, they have not remained in a given local community across a single generation or beyond. Thus, those with an ongoing, transgenerational involvement with particular communities have been far smaller in number than the total populations of those towns or cities.

Furthermore, not all local communities—after having been founded, settled, and builtup—lasted. Some failed, were abandoned, and became "ghost towns." These communities, which like all the others started out to be permanent but were turned into temporary entities, were usually dependent on a single economic resource or were located in heavily rural settings that suffered a large decline in the farming population.

When viewed in a broad historical perspective, the awareness that there have been significant numbers of rural and transient people and abandoned towns would appear to diminish the otherwise evident importance of local place communities to the lives of North Americans. It is important to understand, however, that both the rural and transient populations have needed access to community, even if they haven't lived in one, or at least haven't lived in one for very long. It is apparent that the truly rural population has formed rural neighborhoods, with bits of "community" scattered here and there: a church, a schoolhouse, a market, a mill, a courthouse—structures often used for a variety of purposes. This suggests that, although farmers typically chose to live out on their farms, they still needed the kinds of services that settled communities usually provided and even made efforts to provide those services in an informal way, close to hand. Similarly, the transients, although they did not stay in a particular locality for long, still attached themselves to towns and cities, however temporarily, thus revealing their need for community.

So engrained was the need for access to the benefits of community (even if you didn't want to live or stay in one) that whenever Americans have been outside settled community life, with its politically defined rules, they have created their own forms of community. They did so in order to deal in practical ways with the problems created by people brought together because of common activities or interests. For example, when small groups migrated along well-defined trails over the high plains to particular resource-rich locations in the Rockies or the Pacific (from the 1820s to the 1860s), they created "wagon trains," a kind of temporary, moving community. Such groups composed constitutions, elected councils and captains, organized various tasks, and developed procedures for dealing with those who broke the rules. A more modern version of the wagon train is the mobile home or trailer park, temporary settlements for people moving about in vehicles also used as homes.

Similarly, during the 1840s, 1850s, and 1860s, "squatters" in the Mississippi River Valley and miners in the Rocky Mountains formed another type of temporary community, the "claims club." Both groups settled out ahead of organized government, wrote constitutions, and developed judicial procedures for dealing with those who failed to stake their land or mining claims according to proper procedures. The miners also built mining camps, many of which were short-lived, jerry-built communities.[2] Even the camp revival meetings held by evangelical ministers during the eighteenth and nineteenth centuries took on some of the attributes of temporary communities. Sometimes lasting for a number of days, such gatherings were organized spatially into "streets" lined with tent houses and a "central square" with a preacher's podium and a pit for repentant sinners.[3]

And so, during the course of the nineteenth century, Americans began to form place communities that either weren't meant to be permanent (the wagon train, the claims club, the mining camp, the camp revival) or didn't turn out to be permanent (the ghost town). This happened at a time when large numbers of the population were geographically mobile and/or living in rural areas, outside of a cohesive community context of any kind.

The process whereby Americans came to perceive community as involving more than fixed, permanent place communities thus began in the nineteenth century, when significant portions of the population experienced such communities either from the outside or, if inside, on a temporary basis. Since that time, this process has been greatly enhanced by the enlargement in the scale by which modern life is organized, an enlargement made possible by developments in communication and transportation. With every aspect or dimension of their lives increasingly organized on a scale beyond that of the localities where they actually live, it has become progressively easier for Americans to affiliate with their other forms of identity, to the point that their community is becoming indistinguishable from all the other groups and institutions they belong to.

Community came to mean more than one's town or city when ordinary Americans began to accept statistical categories as a basis for identifying groups. During the nineteenth century, statistics, or "state-istics," were developed by agencies of the various levels of government in the American federal system as a mathematically precise way of measuring important characteristics of the population being governed. Censuses and other statistical reports became increasingly common. Scholars in universities and colleges increased the sophistication by which such investigations could be made. Economic firms and social institutions also used or applied statistics-based research.

Insurance agencies established the first widespread use of statistical categorization in the nineteenth century when they created "categories of risk": for purposes of insuring lives against calamity, everyone was placed in a group on the basis of the likelihood of an accident or an illness. In the early twentieth century, the military developed "I.Q." tests, which, when used more broadly by the educational system, became the basis for "categories of intelligence." And, by the mid-twentieth century, the federal government routinely issued reports on the wealth of Americans, dividing them into "categories of income." In recent decades, Americans have become quite used to associating themselves, in matters as fundamental as intellect and class, wholly on the basis of statistical categorizations.

These statistical "communities" created by governmental and private agencies are appropriate to a modern society whose population increasingly resides in urban settings, filled with strangers, and whose life patterns exist on a continentwide or even global scale. Statistical communities are attenuated, thinned-out communities defined not by place but by category. One is a member of them whether or not one wants to be, or even if one is aware of being a member. While attenuated, statistical communities can be an important form of communal association for those who belong to them. They are mental abstractions that nonetheless relate to real groups of people. In addition, they are artificially limited in spatial or territorial terms by the governmental agency that has created them to various levels of political communities (the nation, a state, a county, a city, or a town), or to a firm's or institution's customers or users, if the agency is "private" in nature.[4]

Another form of even more recently perceived and designated "community" is that of the workplace or the consumption place—plants, office complexes, shopping centers, malls, industrial parks—or that of social institutional settings—including universities and hospitals. These "communities" share with old-fashioned place communities a specific location, one within a town or a city, and so in one sense are smaller than place communities. But if the workplace or consumption place or social institution is affiliated hierarchically with a larger organization, such as a corporation or a federated university system, then these "communities" are greater in scale than a town or a city and can be multilocational.

Membership in a workplace, a consumption place, or a social institution tends be one dimensional, however. Do you work there? Do you have the financial means to purchase something there? Do you have the intelligence to be admitted? Are you genuinely sick or wounded? As communities, some of these organizations are small enough for an individual to know of everyone (as in a town), but many others are large and filled with strangers (as in a city). Others tend to have long-term or "permanent" members (workplaces), but others tend to have transient, short-term members (consumption places) or at least a mixture of the two. The attitude of individuals toward their membership in such communities varies enormously, but where one works, shops, learns, and heals is quite fundamental to one's life, and Americans have with increasing frequency referred to all these places as communities that they belong to.

Like statistical communities, these institutional communities are an appropriate byproduct of modern society, with its large-scale organizations and typically urban settings. An urbanized population seeks smaller contexts in which to gain an identity that is more meaningful to their individual lives. They do so by adding to their ever-spreading, urbanized "place" community a more contained and better defined "place," whether it be for work or consumption or social services.[5]

Yet another recently perceived and designated form of community is the group community, whether it be based on race, ethnicity, sexuality, gender, age, class, occupation, or religion—all the ways people living in modern society divide themselves. Some of these groups have evoked a far deeper sense of identity and loyalty than others, but all either have or will in the future think of themselves as "communities." Racial, ethnic, and religious groupings have evoked the most deep-seated forms of identification, but occupation, and, most recently, gender and sexuality and age have also begun to matter deeply.

Such communities are primarily local, for these social groupings form on the basis of particular place communities in association with given towns and cities, usually defined politically. In the face of the anonymity of urban life, the members of these "group" communities desire a town-like awareness of all the others in the local setting who share their identity. But given the large-scale organizational structures of modern society, all these locally based communities are affiliated with much larger organizations and sometimes participate in activities involving similarly constituted groups elsewhere.

And so, ordinary Americans have come to be associated with communities of various kinds during the course of the twentieth century. Individuals in our contemporary mass society are enveloped by a cocoon of communities, as numerous as the number of significant groups or institutions with which they identify, and to which they belong. In our contemporary, urbanized world, the lone individual, surrounded by strangers though he or she may be, is at the same time linked to an array of "communities" of a political, economic, social, and cultural/intellectual character. Modern life has undoubtedly produced forms of alienation in a crowded human context of strange and unfamiliar people, but it has also made it important for individuals to seek forms of community beyond their "place" community, as many communities as there are forms of identity for these individuals.

It is deeply ironic that ordinary people have applied the historians' most basic concept—community—to all the forms of social identity that they experience as individuals, whereas academic scholars themselves have so restricted their application of the concept that they continue to divide the human past into rigidly divided, politically defined national fields of study. School systems around the world present to their students the nation's past. School teachers and professors continue to instill in the young the sense that history is about the nation and about political life, even though people now routinely think of community as applying to many facets of their lives, facets of varying forms and shapes and sizes.

It is time for historians to break loose from their own rigidly held traditions and to bring about a much-needed synchronization between the way community is treated in formal historical study and the way it is perceived by the public that historians should be serving far more effectively than they have. Just as amateur local historians had the "folk" wisdom to focus on local communities when they were the most important form of community, so now ordinary citizens have broadened what they understand by the term *community* to fit the changed, complex character of modern life. In both cases, academic scholars have had to run to catch up with the more insightful perceptions of the lay public.

Are these newer forms of community as important or as good as the older place communities? These are vitally important questions, but they are questions that I as a historian am unequipped to answer. It certainly can be argued that the loss of the primacy of the town as a small local place community is a momentous human calamity. The town provided a small-scale communal setting for its inhabitants in which the familiar and the known predominated. The recent, rampant urbanization of the world's population has left most individuals in large-scale settings in which the strange and unfamiliar predominate. This, it can be argued, has been a colossal human tragedy. If so, it is very likely that it is an irreversible tragedy. Human beings have reacted to urbanization by redefining community. It is incumbent on academic historians to change the nature of formal historical study to take account of that redefinition.

IV

HISTORIANS AND GENERALIZATIONS

9

Problems in Historical Synthesizing

What follows is not an overall interpretation of historical study today, but rather a highly selective one. I am not concerned here with many dimensions of how scholars examine the past, with—for example—the reliability of evidence, the quality of historical analysis, the nature of historical reality, and the ultimately philosophical character of all historical probings. Instead, I am concerned about two, related problems that historians, especially those who are synthesizers, have not hitherto effectively dealt with or indeed even adequately recognized: (1) the problem of how to establish "fields" or units of historical study that are valid and justifiable, and (2) the problem of how to deal with all aspects of a people's past within a single chronological framework. I am also concerned about the failure of synthesizers to probe the past by applying particular clusters of questions that they share with scholars in adjoining humanistic disciplines, questions that are basic to an understanding of human life but that cut across the traditional historical categories—political, economic, social, cultural-intellectual.

So, what I am investigating are particular problems and questions that are especially germane to those historians, students, and readers alike who are interested in historical synthesis. In the units that follow, I maintain (1) that the only wholly valid and satisfying unit of study is humanity itself and, therefore, that the global perspective is the most revealing one for the investigation of any historical subject, (2) that different, separate, overlapping time frames are required for all aspects of humanity's past when presented in chronological form, and (3) that posing, in addition, a wide variety of basic historical questions deepens and broadens historical synthesis.

WHO?: THE PROBLEM OF FIELDS OR UNITS

Wherever and whenever there has been government, those who have provided syntheses of the past have typically focused on it in their written accounts. This has been the case whether the state in question has been a city, a nation, an empire, or a confederation of nations. Governments have always exercised authority over the people they represent, whether legitimately or by usurpation or conquest. Acting on behalf of people within a certain territory, governments are coercive in that their judicial and armed personnel enforce the laws when they are broken and are rule-making in that their legislators make the laws by which people are governed.

Governments have been the best recordkeepers, challenged by churches, family elites, and corporations, but, as public instrumentalities, they have been more apt to compile, preserve, and make accessible those records. Since the early nineteenth century, historians of the modern world have served as helpmates of nationalism by producing studies of the past confined to nation-states. Fields of study in the developing public school systems included national history, so that generations of school children have been inculcated with various versions of their nation's past. At the same time, nationalist sentiment among adults has strengthened, alongside marked growth in national power. The result has been that ordinary citizens commonly link "history" with its obvious public, political, and national dimensions. As national governments have fostered the growth of nationalism over the past two centuries, they have indirectly shaped prevailing perceptions of modern history itself by predisposing patriotic historians, students, and readers alike to view that past within national and political contexts.

The fundamental problem and danger with such an emphasis is that it seriously distorts historical reality, trying as it does to fit the maelstrom that is human life within national boundaries. The fact is that individuals throughout history have had multiple allegiances and loyalties and identities—through families, local communities, rural and urban neighborhoods, and religious, ethnic, racial, class, occupational, gender, sexual, and age groups. National or political affiliation is only one such affiliation, although, to be sure, an increasingly powerful one in modern times.

But the national/political perspective as the basis for historical study obscures as well as illuminates. For all the power modern national governments have come to exercise, the fact remains that no aspect of human life has existed simply along national political boundaries: not language, not thought, not art, not economic activity, not social class structure, not religion, not architecture, not science or medicine, not sport or recreation, not towns or cities. National governments have affected all of these human activities and ways of living, but they have not made any of them distinctive and unique to particular, territorially defined states.

Why should one aspect of human life determine how humanity is divided and studied historically? The argument in favor of according politics this preeminence is that people identify themselves publicly in a legal and coercive way with their political arrangements, allowing governments to establish and maintain rules and to punish those who disobey them. In this view, the public life of any group is coterminous with governmental activity. Therefore, the only valid history is past politics.

The proponents of this argument tend to ignore the evidence that governments have not continuously dealt with certain aspects of life. In some cases, people have believed that certain matters are too basic to warrant political interference or alteration. In other cases, particular issues or controversies have been so politically divisive as to be ignored by government as a possible threat to its continued existence. In all cases, something nonpolitical in character is important for its own sake, and not just when it becomes a matter of political controversy.

Furthermore, people have identified themselves in many basic, nonpolitical ways. A person who is, say, a Christian, upper middle-class, white, urban, middle-aged male with an English name is identified in ways at least as important as to say that he is an "American." Each of these labels or categories creates a form of identification—religious, economic, social, ethnic, racial, occupational, age, gender, geographic, demographic, linguistic—at least as fundamental as the political one is.

Political life, by its nature, is not more fundamental than other aspects of life, even if it is public, legal, and coercive. Politics does not determine the rest of life, any more than geography, economic life, social structure, thought, or culture determines politics. Each is an autonomous aspect of human life, influencing and interacting with all the others.

And yet, human beings throughout history—both recorded and preliterate—have always had a tendency to divide themselves into groups, into "we's" and "they's," insiders and outsiders, entities whose members share a common awareness, loyalty, and allegiance. The evidence for this is continuous and persistent. Groups have sometimes been in contact with other groups of the same order and scale, which has led to an awareness of differences and similarities, producing friendliness or emulation, hostility or hatred. Some groups have dominated, influenced, controlled, subdued, absorbed, conquered, aided, or protected other groups. Members of particular groups have had their loyalty and allegiance tested by such contacts with others and have variously wavered, disavowed, or reaffirmed their identity, especially in cases in which direct attacks by outsiders force members to defend, fight, and possibly die for their group.

Various groups in human history have been identified by historians, archaeologists, and anthropologists as having awakened significant degrees of loyalty, allegiance, and identification: social groups, such as clans, bands, tribes, and civilizations or those of a feudal, ethnic, racial, or religious character, as well as politically defined groups, such as the inhabitants of city-states, dynastic states, nations, confederacies, and empires. In all cases, the belief on the part of members of particular groups that they were distinctive or unique, whether as superior or inferior to or simply different from other groups of the same character, may later appear to historians as having been distorted or inaccurate. The extent to which these groups have actually known how different or similar the patterns of their lives have been with respect to other groups has varied enormously through the course of human history. But all such groups have shared a predisposition to assume that their life is distinctive. This presumption of distinctiveness has been essential to group identity.

Historians have also discovered cases in which people have shared important characteristics but have nonetheless not usually formed durable, self-conscious groups on the basis of those shared characteristics. I am referring here to class, occupation, gender, sexuality, and age. There is no clear explanation for why a person's ethnic, racial, religious, and political affiliations have so continuously been a basis for powerful group attachments, but not whether a person has been male or female; heterosexual or homosexual; young, middle-aged, or old; in business, the professions, the crafts, or labor; or in the upper, middle, or lower classes.

Age, gender, and sexuality are universal and important human attributes, but, until the recent past, linkage among people on the basis of these characteristics has been hampered by limitations in communication and transportation. The emergence of a youth culture and senior citizens, women's, and homosexual movements are all recent phenomena and are quite limited geographically.

Similarly, class and occupation are important and universal human classifications, even if difficult to define. Yet this fact has not meant that humanity has developed global divisions along occupational and class lines, hampered in this context as well by those same limitations in communication and transportation. Even the emergence of industrial capitalism as a unifying socioeconomic system has not led to a heightened sense of consciousness among people within the same social and economic categories. Rich and powerful elites have sometimes developed a common identity and awareness, but until quite recently have not been groups of an extended geographic kind. Labor movements have usually confined themselves to local, regional, and national contexts, even though industrial capitalism has created the same kinds of labor over vast areas of the globe. Those in specific occupations have for much of the human past created associations of various kinds, but these groups have been limited in size, scope, and durability.

Even in local and regional contexts, however, age, gender, sexuality, class, and occupation have not produced group activity of the intensity that racial, ethnic, and religious identification has. This is the mystery. Why should a person's race, ethnicity, and religion matter more and create a much stronger propensity to produce deep group allegiance than a person's gender, sexuality, age, class, and occupation? In other terms, why should sources of identification based on a person's in-bred kinship groupings (or "ethnicity") and beliefs (or "religiosity") have usually mattered, historically, more than other sources of identification based on a person's demographic composition (gender, sexuality, age) or work (occupation) or position in society (class)?

Political groupings have a special character in that, by definition they are both public and coercive. One's membership in a city-state, nation, or empire involves living under rules or laws and being incarcerated by the state if one misbehaves. But, until recently, with the creation of the United Nations, political groups have not been universal or global, any more than social, economic, or religious groups have been.

Historians of the modern world have focused on the nation-state as the most important group, But although powerful, nations have not ordered and controlled and divided human life along national boundaries. Since the nonpolitical dimensions of humanity's past have not varied on a national political basis, such a perspective is incomplete, and it distorts, exaggerates, or underestimates distinctions within the nonpolitical aspects of life. Economic, social, cultural, and intellectual developments have their own contours, variations, and rates of change and cannot be subsumed within a politically defined world.

Historians of the premodern world have not resolved the problem of defining units or fields of study any more satisfactorily than those who have presented general accounts of the recent past. Whether probing the history of the clans, bands, and tribes of primitive peoples or the city-states, feudal systems, dynastic states, and empires of civilized peoples or the confederacies of either, historians, archaeologists, and anthropologists have failed to define distinctive and unified groups. They have failed for the same reason that modern nations cannot be used as the basis for defining such groups: What defines people politically does not do so linguistically, geographically, economically, socially, culturally, intellectually, recreationally, or religiously.

Ironically, not even those who have recently presented "world" histories have obviated the problem. Even though the global perspective would appear to reduce "units" or "fields" to one—humanity itself—the common practice of dividing world history into the lives of "civilizations" keeps the question of definition alive. The ancient civilizations of Asia (the Mesopotamian, Egyptian, Indian, and Chinese), the later Eurasian (the Graeco-Roman and Islamic) civilizations, and the still later European (or Western) civilization are difficult to define as distinctive and unified entities. There was much variety in each of them, and their defining features have differed from one to the other. The basic bond has sometimes been a common language, sometimes a common religion, and sometimes a common government. Similarly, efforts to define primitive or barbaric peoples—the nomadic or agricultural clans, bands, tribes, confederacies, and empires of Asia, Europe, Africa, and the Americas—involve the same complications.

Such efforts to define "people" also fail to take account of the interpenetration of one people—through migration or conquest—by another. How does a given people occupy a particular territory if it is intermixed with other peoples? By focusing on particular groups, historians present a too static, fixed, and thus distorted probing of the past.

I believe that, rather than define fields or units based on groups, historians should deal with particular historical subjects or aspects of life, either in a global or a localized perspective. I am not willfully ignoring the reality of human groups and the great impact membership in such groups has had on the history of humanity. But to use such groups as units of historical study obfuscates, distorts, and confuses us in our efforts to understand the past, simply because the various dimensions of human life have not usually been organized on the basis of these groups. Varying global and local perspectives are a more revealing basis for exploring any human phenomenon because, by finding out how something existed at a certain time in all its variety throughout the globe, as well as how it took on particular forms at particular localities at a particular time, we can at least try to achieve the fullest possible measure of historical understanding of that phenomenon.

What I am calling for will not basically alter the work of historians who focus on well-delineated subjects in their scholarship, although such scholars should be far more aware of the importance of both the global and the local perspectives than they have been. Such studies will continue to contribute to the work of those who seek wider interpretations. What will be drastically altered if my prescriptions are followed is the nature of historical synthesis. No longer would there be an intellectually justifiable need for historians of groups, be they bands, clans, tribes, ethnic groups, feudal systems, towns, cities, provinces, nations, empires, confederacies, or civilizations. The true work of historical synthesizers, the one history textbook, would be an account or interpretation of the human past, organized on the basis of various aspects of human life. Study of humanity's past would then be what it should be: an explanation of how and why and when a species of being has come to live the way it does now.

I am not so naive as to expect that well-established units of historical study will suddenly disappear or that historians will suddenly cease to synthesize the scholarship that will surely continue to appear within those fields. Such work will doubtless go on for a long time. But I am urging synthesizers and textbook authors to become far more aware than they usually have been of how incomplete their "fields" are, of how many alternative ways there are to divide up humanity for purposes of historical study, of how groups that appear valid for the study of one aspect of human life may not be for other aspects. Hopefully, future synthesizers will gradually become more reflective of and responsive to the vastly complicated nature of the human past.

Synthesizers should become sensitive to the fact that the self-awareness, allegiance, loyalty, and identity that certain groups in human history have possessed have far outstripped their capacity to be distinctive, separate, and unified in reality. The patterns of life developed by humanity, if perceived from a global perspective, have been far more complicated and varied than customary divisions in historical study have hitherto allowed us to recognize. Those who have presented world histories reveal this, though their accounts, focused as they are on ill-defined "civilizations," still contain some of the confusion and distortion that have characterized syntheses and texts on smaller entities. The only clear perspective on human history is the global one, and the most insightful syntheses will be those that interpret various aspects of life—political, economic, social, and cultural-intellectual—on a global basis, indicating variations within the global pattern on whatever localized basis seems appropriate.

WHAT?: THE PROBLEM OF CHRONOLOGIES

A problem closely related to that of units or fields is that of chronologies, the linchpin being government. Just as syntheses of modern history have made national governments the focus for fields based on the nation-state, so too have political developments formed the core of the historical chronologies into which these fields have been organized. Synthesizers and textbook authors have deemed that only governmental activity is worthy of continuous attention, to the point that they have periodized the past according to political events. Even historians of the premodern world have accorded government a central place in accounts of various empires in western, southern, and eastern Asia and in southern and Central Europe and of assorted dynastic kingdoms in Europe, Africa, and Central and South America. Only the world histories that have been based on the study of civilizations have an organizing principle clearly broader than the political aspect of life.

In the public school systems that have emerged since the nineteenth century, ordinary people have been taught that political activity is more historically important than other kinds of human activity. Journalists reinforce this bias by regularly labeling current political events as being of "historic importance."

Yet the political dimension is not inherently more important or more historic than other dimensions, and it certainly distorts our understanding of the past to pretend that it is. One aspect of human life is not more basic than another in the sense that it determines the others. Each aspect interacts with all the others to produce the totality of human life. Distortion comes from partial perspectives. All dimensions need to be examined and interpreted, and the influences of one on another need to be detected.

For those synthesizers who continue to define their subject on the basis of a human group, of whatever size, the people being examined historically (however unsatisfactorily they can be defined as a distinctive entity) need to be studied to discover (1) the values and ideas they have lived by; (2) their understanding of each other and of foreigners or others, of the world around them, and of the nature and purpose of life; (3) the way they have created things; (4) the way they have fed, clothed, and housed themselves; (5) the way they have spent their work time and their leisure time; (6) the way they have governed themselves; (7) the way they have arranged themselves into classes and occupations; (8) the way they have divided into ethnic and racial groups; (9) the way they have interacted with others and with their environment—all the significant aspects of human life need to be interwoven to produce a satisfactory chronology.

Chronologies based on political developments, and divided into political periods are warped and distorted, providing only an incomplete perspective from which to view historical reality and change. To examine the past primarily as matters of political concern is to omit much of significance, even when political life is defined as the public life of a people. For a political system can evade, ignore, and obfuscate developments in other dimensions—as well as illuminate, classify, and deal with or resolve issues arising from those other dimensions. Politics is not, therefore, automatically the central perspective from which to view the past, nor is it reliable.

Significant changes in the structure and function of a political system, specifically in its lawmaking, administrative, and adjudicative aspects, can come suddenly, through revolution or civil war or civil disobedience. Far more often, however, they have come gradually, through slow, evolutionary alterations. Seldom does change coincide with reigns and administrations and dramatic events, although historians have typically used this kind of change as the basis for defining political periods. This has been because synthesizers and textbook writers want to keep historical chronologies easily accessible to ordinary readers and to make their historical accounts personalized and dramatized, offering important and exciting leaders and events as explanations for historical change.

Economic change has almost always been gradual and evolutionary, with the development of new forms—organizations, processes, capital, labor, resources, markets, property, wealth, and ownership—occurring alongside older ones. Economics exhibits certain stages of growth and decline. Revolution has rarely produced important long-term economic change, although war, civil strife, disease, and famine have often had significant short-term impact.

Generally, social change has also been gradual and evolutionary. Social inequality based on class, caste, gender, and age has been a constant feature of all human history. The mix of upper, middle, and lower classes and castes and their nature and size have varied, but they have changed slowly, and lasting change has rarely been the result of revolution.

Cultural and intellectual life has similarly been slow and evolutionary, with older ideas, values, beliefs, and artistic creations coexisting with new ones. Rarely has there been lasting, but sudden and revolutionary cultural or intellectual change.

In one sense, political events and developments differ from all other kinds. Since political activity is by definition public, it has a distinctive historical visibility. In its public aspect, a group is acting, it is doing something, and the historian has a special obligation to take account of such happenings. There is something definite, irreversible, unrepeatable about particular political actions, and the historian is obliged to be as accurate as he or she can be in constructing a chronology of these activities. Groups leave their impress through time and space most visibly in their public actions.

By contrast, economic, social, and cultural-intellectual change is far less clear, less straightforward, less linear. Old and new ways coexist in an overlayered manner. Several adult generations are alive at any given time, and each brings to bear its own somewhat contrasting past experiences and current perceptions. The historical meaning of economic, social, and cultural-intellectual activity is far less evident. The historian must attempt to construct patterns of persistence and change out of a maze of largely repetitious or usually slowly evolving happenings.

Chronologies based on well-defined epochs of any kind are misleading, however, and significantly distort historical reality. The rate and depth of change for each aspect of human life differ from all others. In addition, for politics as much as for other dimensions of life, old ways persist as new ways appear. Dominant forms do not obliterate older, declining ones, and earlier activities, institutions, and behavior patterns remain even while changing their social meaning and importance. Social reality is of a manylayered and textured character, and simple periodization violates its innate complexity.

Therefore, chronological divisions should be left imprecise and certainly overlapping, with varying spans of time for each dimension of life as the chronology moves toward the present. A good analogy here is to layers of sedimentary rock, which are overlaid, but of varying lengths and widths, and obviously connected, but each with its own shape.

So, too, should a single chronology consist of segments of political, economic, social, and cultural-intellectual developments that are of varying lengths, depending on the nature of change in each. Since no aspect of human life controls the extent and rate of change in any other, synthesizers should establish periodization for each on the basis of the contours of change peculiar to each. A certain line of evolution may have run its course in one aspect by a certain date, but that date might mean very little as a dividing point for the periodization of any other aspect of life. The best scheme would be for the synthesizer to proceed from (say) political to economic to social to cultural-intellectual and allow each period to begin and end as seems most appropriate, and then start the sequence over again as many times as necessary to bring the account into the recent past.

Stress should always be placed on the interaction of the various aspects of life with each other. Events and trends, that is, both short- and long-term developments, should be accounted for, and no distinction should be made with respect to emphasis between political events and other kinds of events, or between political trends and other kinds of trends. Particularities and generalizations should always be in balance, with neither predominating. An event is part of a trend, and a trend is made up of events—in all aspects of life, not just the political. The traditional focus on events in historical writing distorts and misleads, and it has persisted as a result of the desire of synthesizers and textbook writers to dramatize the past, making it accessible to ordinary readers.

Synthesizers should become sensitive to the fact that various aspects of human life evolve at their own rate, to their own extent, and in their own way, each interacting with and influencing the others, and none necessarily more basic or determinant than any other. A single chronology with coexisting, overlapping, varying spans of time for each dimension of life is unquestionably the most effective way of organizing a synthesis of the human past.

WHY?: HISTORICAL QUESTIONS

And yet, a history of humanity or any of its subgroups dealing with the political, economic, social, and cultural-intellectual aspects of life organized in a single chronology leaves unanswered basic questions that those in various humanistic academic disciplines have developed. These questions—taken all together—would deepen and broaden historical study if employed within the framework of a single historical account. Used in varied ways by scholars in philosophy, religion, language, the arts, geography, psychology, sociology, economics, and political science, these questions are wider and more profound in what they reveal about human life than does inquiry based on activities (political, economic, social, cultural-intellectual), institutions (schools, churches, corporations, associations, governments, and so on), and groups (lawyers, doctors, clergymen, professors and teachers, farmers, laborers of various kinds, and so on).

All together, these questions constitute a much-needed addition to the single, varied chronology that any well-constructed account of the past should start with. The apparent overlapping and repetition that would ensue would be more than compensated for by the great gain in insight into the character of the human past.

I am not suggesting that historians have ignored these questions, but that they have been extremely uneven in the extent to which they have focused on them. Some have already been much studied; others have been investigated in a partial or skewed way; and still others have only recently begun to be used as a basis for historical study. Historians have been academic magpies for a long time, ransacking the work of colleagues in related humanistic and social scientific disciplines for methods, theories, and concepts that have seemed valid or workable, given the historical evidence available. I am taking what has hitherto been a random process one step further by providing in what follows a comprehensive and systematized list of questions that are of basic concern to scholars in many different disciplines. I have attempted throughout to frame the questions in terms that will make the most sense to historians in particular.

I am suggesting that a "part two" be appended to any synthetic work that embraces a field or unit of study and that this additional part consist of a thorough examination of all the questions that follow. I have not attempted to rate the questions in terms of their relative importance, for I believe that the value of introducing such a new part to works of synthesis lies in the totality of what can be said about the entire list. Just as chronologies and fields of study should be as comprehensive as it is possible to make them, so, too, should investigations of this kind.

These questions, as designed, sometimes embrace polarities or opposing characteristics and are best encountered in clusters, that is, in groupings of related lines of inquiry. By referring to the population, I leave it to individual synthesizers to define who is within the group about whom they choose to write a general historical account. (If, as I suggest, the population were to be humanity itself, references in the questions to such terms as "others" and "outsiders" and "emigrants" and "immigrants" would have to be redefined to fit within a global context.)

CLUSTER I

1. LIBERTY/TYRANNY— Who had liberty and freedom? What forms did they take? Who was denied them? What forms did tyranny take? Who was

enslaved? What forms did slavery take? To what extent did those without liberty or freedom accept or resist their condition?

2. EQUALITY/INEQUALITY—Who was equal? What forms did equality take? Who was excluded? Was there social, economic, and political equality? To what extent did those who were unequal accept or resist their condition?

3. JUSTICE/INJUSTICE—What was justice? Were all treated fairly and equally under the law or with reference to prevailing religious beliefs, basic values, and ideals? Who was treated unjustly? How were the law-breakers brought to justice? How were they rehabilitated? Did the population act outside the law to maintain the law, that is, through extralegal means and agencies?

4. DEMOCRATIC/AUTHORITARIAN—How democratic/ authoritarian were the political, economic, social, cultural, intellectual, and religious arrangements of life? Did the extent of democracy and authoritarianism vary from one of these dimensions of life to another?   Did democracy and authoritarianism increase or decrease over time, or were they of a cyclical character?

5. POWER/IMPOTENCE—Who had power? Was it centralized or diversified? Did it matter which individuals or groups exercised it? What was its relationship to wealth?   What form did the various types of power—political, economic, social, cultural, intellectual, religious—take? What were the forms of social control used by those in power? Was there a tendency to dominate other people outside of the population, through imperialism or colonialism? Whom did those in positions of power victimize, and what forms of impotency were created thereby? What kinds of symbiotic relationships existed between those with power and those who were victimized or rendered impotent to any extent?

6. WEALTH/POVERTY—Who was wealthy? How did they obtain, sustain, and increase their wealth? What forms did their power and influence take? Did those with wealth change or persist from generation to generation? Who was poor? To what extent did the poor accept or resist their condition? Was wealth or property private or public, individually or communally owned, or both? Was wealth concentrated or spread out? What was the prevailing attitude toward wealth and poverty?

7. CLASS/CASTE—How well defined were social classes? Was there a ruling class? Who was in it? Did it change or persist in character from one generation to another? Did its values and perceptions dominate the way

others perceived the world? How hierarchical or mobile was the population? Was there a caste, as well as a class, system? How were the status and the characteristics of particular classes and castes defined? By whom?

CLUSTER II

8. VALUES—What were the basic values (religious and secular) of the population? What were the prevailing, largely unexamined, unassailable assumptions? What were the ideals, goals, and principles that ordered and gave value to life? What was the good life, that is, good society, good government, and good economy? What was basic, as opposed to ephemeral or subsidiary? Did these values persist or change over time?

9. LEGITIMACY—Under what circumstances did something attain legitimacy, that is, the unquestioned right to exist, the standard against which other, similar things were measured, were seen to be bogus? For example: status, wealth, power, class, values, beliefs, personal and social behavior.

10. NORMALITY/ABNORMALITY—What was normality, normal behavior, sanity? What groups and institutions defined and enforced it? How were those who behaved abnormally or who were insane treated?

11. DISSENT/CONFORMITY—Was criticism or opposition to prevailing patterns of life allowed or encouraged or forbidden? Who were the critics and dissenters, and what forms did their criticisms and dissent take? What forms did conformity take? How did the population arrive at an orthodox value, belief, pattern of activity, behavior?

12. MAJORITIES/MINORITIES—Who were the minorities? How were they treated by the majority? Were there powerful and wealthy minorities as well as poor and powerless ones, that is, minorities at the top as well as on the bottom? Did the majority have a strong sense of itself? How much power and wealth did it have? Did its values and beliefs prevail?

13. IMMIGRATION/EMIGRATION—Who were the immigrants and the emigrants? What problems did they create? What did they contribute to the life of the population? To what extent were they regarded and treated as outsiders? When did they cease to be so regarded and treated by the native-born portion of the population?

CLUSTER III

14. UNITY—Was the population unified in its political, economic, social, cultural, intellectual, and religious life, or was it characterized by its decentralized, fragmented character? Did it have a strong sense of identity and loyalty? Did its unity have institutional, symbolic, psychological, emotional, and mental dimensions? Did its unity lead to a belief in superiority over other people? What forms did disunity take? Was there notable controversy, strife, division, hostility, debate, violence, warfare?

15. UNIQUENESS—Was the population unique in all the dimensions of its life? Did it have its own forms of language, art, philosophy, religion, science, technology, economy, social structure, leisure-time and recreational activity, ethnic/racial definition, political system? If it was, in reality, like those of other peoples, how did it attain a sense of its own identity?

16. STABILITY/INSTABILITY—Was the population characterized more by its stability or by its instability? What forms did stability and instability take? Was there rebellion/civil war/ revolution/civil unrest? What was the role of the police and the armed services in maintaining order? What were the forms of repression, of social control? What were the instrumentalities for the transmission of power, wealth, and prevailing values from one generation to another? To what extent was there social and geographic mobility?

17. PERSISTENCE/CHANGE—Did the patterns of life persist without major change over long periods of time? Who or what caused change? Was it progressive or cyclical or regressive? Did change come as a result of internal controversy, division, strife, hostility, debate, or through encounters with others? Was change the result of reform, revolution, or uneventful, long-term developments? To what extent did change come as a result of the actions of the famous and the powerful, and to what extent by the individual or collective actions of ordinary people? Did change come as a result of altering conditions in the environment, in the natural world?

CLUSTER IV

18. VIOLENCE/PEACE—Were the people especially violent or pacifistic? Did this persist or change over time? What forms did pacifism take? Why did violence erupt among the people (in the form of crime) or among them and other people (in the form of war)? What forms did violent crime and warfare take?

19. LOVE/HATE—Was the population characterized by its fraternity, civility, and benevolence, or by its rudeness, incivility, hate, sexual exploitation, social indifference, and racial/ethnic/class prejudice?

20. HAPPINESS/SADNESS—Was the population characterized by its satisfactions—its sense of integration, contentment, joy, humor, optimism—or by its dissatisfactions—its sense of alienation, stress, restlessness, joylessness, humorlessness, pessimism?

CLUSTER V

21. TIME—How did the population conceive of time: on a daily, seasonal basis or on a horological basis (clock time)? Was time perceived as progressive, regressive, cyclical, or static? What effects did these definitions have on the nature of work and leisure and ceremony, on the population's natural world, and on the purpose and direction of life itself?

22. WORK/LEISURE—How was work or labor defined? What did it mean to work well or badly? What was the prevailing attitude toward the products and services of labor with reference to quality, durability, beauty, and satisfaction? Was work organized by clock time or daily/seasonal time? Was work time-oriented or task-oriented? What were the contractual, legal arrangements of labor, that is, the varying degrees of free and slave labor? Was there a sharp dividing line between work and leisure or play? Did the population have a well-developed imagination or sense of play, of fantasy? What did leisure-time activities—play, games, recreation, entertainment, artistic activity—reveal about the prevailing values and preoccupations of the population? Were those who worked in leisure-time activities—athletes, entertainers, artists—highly regarded?

23. SPACE/GEOGRAPHY/ENVIRONMENT/NATURE—What were the characteristics of the geography the population lived in? In what ways did the physical setting influence the kind of political, economic, and social system that developed? How did the population perceive the natural world and its place in it? How did the population relate to its environment, to its water and land and the plants, animals, and minerals on and in them? Was the population's life in harmony or disharmony with the life cycles and rhythms of the natural world? Did the population characteristically want more space; that is, did it have a tendency to be politically or territorially expansionist? How did the population's geographical position in the world affect its relations with others? What was the relationship of land and water to wealth? Were there important natural disasters?

24. MATERIAL CULTURE—What did the human-made, artifactual world consist of? What does it reveal about the life of the people? What was the prevailing attitude toward technology? What was the role of science, medicine, communications, transportation, and warfare in the development of technology? What was the impact of technology on the population and on its environment? Was the population technologically innovative, backward, quick to copy? How were products distributed, bought and sold, exchanged, traded?

25. SENSES—What did the population's world look like, sound like, smell like, taste like, feel like? What does this reveal about the character of life then?

CLUSTER VI

26. COMMUNICATIONS—Did the population communicate in a language understood by all? Did language reveal class, power, wealth? Did the forms of communication that developed lead to understanding or misunderstanding among the population? In what ways were body gestures and movements, colors and lines, sculpted objects, musical sounds, and numbers used as other forms of communication beyond verbal communication?

27. TRUTH/KNOWLEDGE—Did the population value truth and knowledge? What forms did the search for truth and knowledge take? Did the educational system give primacy to the search? Did the population live by truthful and knowledgeable assessments of itself or by delusions, distortions, and lies? In what ways were those who sought truth and knowledge critical of the prevailing patterns of life and of the predominant values? In what ways did notions of truth and knowledge change over time? Did different elements in the population adhere to different forms of truth and knowledge?

28. HONESTY/HYPOCRISY—To what extent did the population attempt to live by its ideals, or to resolve discrepancies between its ideals and reality? Were the public and private utterances of the population notable for their honest revelations or for their inflations and distortions?

29. BEAUTY/FASHION—What did craftsmen, designers, artists, and creators of all kinds consider to be aesthetically of value? Did what they considered to be aesthetically of value change over time? To what extent did the population value aesthetically oriented creations? What was fashionable, in "good taste"? Did what was fashionable change slowly or rapidly over time? In what ways did fashion relate to class, wealth, power?

30. EXCELLENCE—What was considered to be excellent or of quality? Did this standard change over time? Was the population characterized by the place it gave to excellence or quality or by the place it gave to mediocrity and the average?

CLUSTER VII

31. INDIVIDUAL—How important was the individual? Was a single human life highly valued? How important were particular individuals in shaping the life of the population? Did it matter that they, as unique individuals, were in positions of power, influence, and wealth at particular times and places? How did an individual, whether famous or ordinary, perceive and live life?

32. MALES/FEMALES—Did males and females have sharply defined and separated spheres or roles? Which sex was dominant? Was that dominance fixed, cyclical, progressive, or regressive?

33. LIFE CYCLE—How were the phases of life perceived? How did an individual's phase of life determine the place he had in the population?

34. HEALTH/DISEASE—Did the population tend to be healthy and long-lived, rapidly increasing in numbers, or the opposite? Was disease epidemic or endemic? Was the food supply adequate or inadequate? How were the sick and handicapped treated?

35. FAMOUS/HEROIC—Who, what sort of person, became famous? What does this tell us about the population's values and priorities and preoccupations? What did the heroic consist of? Who became folk heroes, mythologized leader figures? What does this sense of the heroic tell us about the population's values, priorities, and preoccupations?

36. SUCCESS/FAILURE—What were the attributes of a successful life? Did these attributes persist or change over time? Who—what groups and institutions—defined what constituted success? What was the impact of failure on individuals and groups in the population?

37. DEATH—What were the ceremonies and perceptions of death? What do they reveal about the population's attitudes toward life itself?

CLUSTER VIII

38. FAMILY—Was the family nuclear or extended? Was it hierarchical,

authoritarian, or patriarchal/matriarchal, or was it democratic? What was the role of the family in the life of the population? How did family life influence political, economic, social, cultural, intellectual, and religious life?

39. PRIVATE/PUBLIC—Was there a clear line of division between what was private and what was public? Did this line change over time? What was the role or place of government in the life of the population? What aspects of life were beyond the reach of government? What was purely private? Was a clear distinction made between the "state" and individuals and groups?

40. COMMUNITY—How did the population define its communities? What does this definition reveal about the values and priorities and preoccupations of the population? Was that which was communalistic in form more or less important than that which was individualistic in form? Which form and level of community was the most successful, durable, persistent, important?

41. CHARACTER—What were the outstanding characteristics of the population; that is, what was its overall personality profile? Did this profile persist or change over time? Did all groups in the population share these characteristics, or just dominant ones?

CONCLUSION

History is already one of the most synthetic of academic disciplines. Only anthropology and journalism share its breadth. The study of the past involves the entire life of humanity, not just its political, economic, social, cultural, intellectual, religious aspects. But historians as a group have become specialists, masters, it is often said, of more and more about less and less. Every active historical scholar lives a dichotomous existence: as a professor of a broadly synthetic discipline, but as a scholar who is usually a narrowly trained specialist. Since the nineteenth century, academic elites all over the "West" have undergone a process of professionalization and specialization, a development that has affected historians as much as any other group.

But, in my view, this development makes the work of synthesis, of drawing together and finding meaning in the great outpouring of academic scholarship, a vital and significant task. If this scholarship is to have relevance to the population at large, it must be conveyed in broad, synthetic accounts that draw together the results of multitudinous probings of extremely particularized subjects. What I have said here is an effort to improve the nature of historical synthesis. Such efforts have hitherto lacked rigor and precision and breadth in both their definition and in their content, a condition that has unnecessarily limited their effectiveness.

10

False Generalizations in
Historical Writing

I would like to concentrate here on two of the various ways that academic historical writing produces false generalizations. One is the practice—widely indulged in by historians, editors, and publishers alike—of creating greatly inflated titles and conclusions for articles and books, a practice that involves generalizing far beyond the actual evidence the author has examined. The other is for historians to use evidence statistically and thereby to produce faceless averages that don't describe or explain real individuals who have actually lived and died.

Academic historical writing, like academic writing in general, focuses on interpretations, analyses, syntheses, concepts, and models that provide us with complex and sophisticated meanings for social reality. Going beyond the empiricism of amateur historians, who have usually been concerned about their own lives or their own communities and not about wider patterns of life, academic historians seek large and deep meanings for their subjects of inquiry. Scholars have tried to find the very patterns amateurs have eschewed. Academic studies are typically presented as a basis for valid generalizations, even though their authors have usually examined only a portion, often a very small portion, of the subject examined. Moreover, these scholarly generalizations are often based on evidence used statistically, a process that turns actual individuals into faceless abstractions and averages.

The only true reality for each of us is the experiences of our own lives. Encased in our own minds and bodies, we are unchangeably separate from all other humans. Our efforts to generalize about others, about human life or human groups, will always be blurred and distorted because we live irreducibly separate lives and can't directly experience social reality in the way that we experience our own lives. Nevertheless, the only perspective from which we can understand social reality is from our vantage point as autonomous individuals. The only meaningful way each of us can understand life in any of its forms is to observe it in the only way we can live it, as individuals. This Aristotelian as well as existential sense of reality is far more persuasive to me than a Platonic emphasis on concepts, models, categories, or forms.

Amateur historians are natural empiricists. For them, particular individuals and towns, cities, and nations are real: the category of humanity or town or city or nation means very little. The fundamental problem with academic thinking is that it involves generalizations about categories of being that exist only in the human mind, relegating to secondary importance the fact that all of these categories consist of individuals who themselves are what is real. Even academically produced "biographical" studies of particular persons, communities, institutions, or groups are presented for what they can tell us about the categories to which they belong. What sort of person, what kind of city or nation, what manner of an ethnic or racial or class group or social organization? How does a case study illuminate its category or phenomenon?

The result has been that academic studies usually find more meaning, discern more of a pattern, and project more understanding than is actually the case. Social reality will always be poorly comprehended by such existentially separated minds as we humans possess. This is so even with the strenuous efforts social scientists have made to produce methodologies that reduce human social activity to the predictable patterns that natural scientists used to think they had found in the physical world around us. Collective human behavior is too complicated, too variegated, and subject to too many variables for any academic methodology to encompass it. Even more importantly, human beings experience, remember, or predict a given moment in time and space in uniquely different ways and can never be expected to agree on a particular rendering of social reality of any kind. No method can overcome this irrevocable, irreducible distinction in the way that individuals experience reality.

And yet, academic historians—like other scholars—have invested their studies with meaning by making generalizations that are by nature tentative and idiosyncratic. Historians do this because of their engrained habit of seeking larger patterns in the collective or social life of individual human beings. It is natural for persons academically trained to seek meaning in generalizations. It is also good for other humans to be aware of these efforts to interpret their collective behavior. What is amiss here is that academics claim too much! In an effort to justify their work's utility to the larger population, they have ascribed to it a larger value than it usually deserves, a greater precision than it often has, and a higher level of understanding than it actually possesses. What the whole academic enterprise badly needs is a much greater degree of humility on the part of its practitioners, a much franker admission on their part that scholarly efforts to grasp social reality are inherently limited and never final.

Inflated titles and the reduction of humans to statistical averages are two large manifestations of the widespread tendency among academic historians and other kinds of scholars to overgeneralize from their research.

The most obvious indication of overgeneralizing, with regards to a book or an article, is the rampant practice, indulged in by editors, publishers, and authors themselves, of entitling a published work in a way that implies that the author has examined in depth far more than he or she actually has. This is a profoundly revealing practice. It is the most obvious indication we have that all the parties to the production of a piece of academic writing feel that it is important to establish range in the work being published, lest potential readers be put off by an excessively narrow line of inquiry and fail to generate sufficient interest to examine or read or purchase the piece. As the evidence used by academic historians has proliferated, as the subjects they study have grown rapidly, and as their methodologies and techniques have multiplied, lone scholars—even those working with a partner or a team—are unable to examine a given historical subject in sufficient depth to achieve academic respectability.

Synthesizers such as myself are painfully aware that our knowledge of a given historical subject is most tentative; that the articles and monographs that deal with aspects of it are varied; and that such writings are uneven in coverage and in the persuasiveness of their author's evidence, methodology, and interpretation. As academic historians, reflecting scholarly activity throughout the university, have mastered more and more about less and less, they collectively feel the need to make a claim for a wider mastery than they actually possess. In so doing, they seek to avoid the oblivion that would come from being so specialized that there would be no one who cared enough or knew enough to appreciate their work.

Examples of inflated titles in well-established fields of historical study, such as my own field of American history, abound. The typical procedure is for a scholar (1) to select as a subject a phenomenon of large-scale dimensions, but (2) to choose a particular locality—a town or a city, or even several towns or cities or counties—or, more specifically, a sample from the populations or institutions of such communities as the "database," and then (3) to make some observations or reach some conclusions about their subject based on their research, but also (4) to compare their findings to those of other scholars who have worked on the same subject as it applies to other localities, and, finally, (5) to select a title and to make conclusions that convey to readers that the resulting study contributes to our understanding of the general phenomenon that the scholar has selected for investigation.

For instance, a number of scholars have studied Lynn or Lowell or the Merrimac Valley in Massachusetts and have sought to make widely applicable observations about the industrialization process. See, for example, Alan Dawley, *Class and Community: The Industrial Revolution in Lynn*[1]; Paul Faler, *Mechanics and Manufacturers in the Early Industrial Revolution: Lynn, Massachusetts, 1780–1860*[2]; Thomas Dublin, *Women at Work: The Transformation of Work and Community in Lynn, Massachusetts, 1826–1860*[3]; and Mary H. Blewett, *Men, Women, and Work: Class, Gender, and Protest in the New England Shoe Industry, 1780–1910*[4] (which actually deals only with Essex County, the county in Massachusetts that includes some of the Merrimac Valley).

Notice how each main title refers to a subject of vast proportions but how each subtitle reveals how limited the actual demographic or institutional research base really was. I am not singling out Alan Dawley, Paul Faler, Thomas Dublin, and Mary Blewett for engaging in scholarly practices that their fellow scholars regard as reprehensible. On the contrary, these able historians have produced highly regarded and well-known academic studies. They have done well what their professional colleagues esteem.

My point is that in all of the above instances, and in countless others, the author's title does not accurately reflect his or her much more limited research or database. The author's thesis, conclusions, and major observations (try as he or she has to link his or her findings to those of other scholars) are presented as having a wider validity than his or her actual research warrants.

Even those scholars who have written on subjects of national dimensions from the perspective of national governments or other institutions often entitle their studies in such a way that they purport to have covered something far broader than is allowed by their particular evidence, which often involves sampling of various kinds.

A second manifestation of academic historians' and other scholars' deeply engrained tendency to overgeneralize is the widespread practice of rendering all kinds of evidence statistically. In this way, the human beings so examined are reduced to faceless averages, to beings without a specific identity. This practice also mars our understanding of the human past because, once the people we study or try to recall are turned into identity-less creatures, into numerical generalizations of one kind or another, we lose the only reality there is: the existence of particular individuals who also act in a social setting.

Groups statistically analyzed by historians can be identified as belonging to a certain language, religion, occupation, ethnicity, class, gender, sexuality, and age grouping. Historians usually try to determine how often or how typically persons belonging to certain categories act or behave in a certain way, advocate a certain point of view, make a particular kind of decision, or participate in an event in a prescribed manner. But such historians have never been able to demonstrate that persons who share a given statistical profile, who belong to the same categories, necessarily act and behave and believe in the same manner. Individuals and circumstances vary too much for human life to be successfully reduced to formulaic connections between the categories individuals belong to and their behavior, actions, and beliefs. The argument that tendencies can be determined between categories of identity and resulting behavior, activity, and belief is of greatly limited value because tendencies don't explain an individual human being's life. Analysis that rests on the discovery of tendencies doesn't go very far as a revelation of social reality in past time.

Historians now routinely use the great array of documentary and artifactual evidence in several ways. Most of the evidence is of a visual character. Aural evidence is much rarer but is becoming more common: recorded interviews, taped conversations, sound tracks and so on. Historians typically produce books whose contents are mainly written texts with notes, but that sometimes contain illustrations of various kinds of visual evidence, such as maps, prints, paintings, and photographs. Historians much more rarely produce historical (visual) films or (aural) tapes.

Whatever the medium or whatever the mix of sources, only one kind of evidence strongly tends to reduce real historical individuals to abstractions. That is *statistical evidence*, the material that appears in charts, graphs, and lists within historical writings. Maps, prints, paintings, photographs, interviews, reminiscences, letters, speeches, records, reports, newspapers, archaeological remains—all are directly linked to actual human beings who have particular identities that can be described or depicted in detailed ways. It is when historians (and others, even those who produce the evidence in the first place) seek to render such evidence statistically, and thus to generalize about the human beings dealt with, that historical sources become the basis for abstractions, and not for information about particular individuals. Statistics that are used in order to make generalizations, such as how typical, how often, and how many, by their very nature produce abstractions.

Evidence used to illustrate observations is also used by academic scholars, but without statistical renderings, their studies lack a suitable basis for generalization, which is above all else what they want to achieve. Otherwise, their work is criticized for being anecdotal and impressionistic, without a sound basis for an overall interpretation of their subject. However graced with illustrated material (material, it must be said, of ever greater variety and profusion), academic scholarship lacks respectability if the author's generalizations are not regularly buttressed with the one way of rendering evidence in a form on which sound generalizations can be made: statistics. Thus, numerical formulations have become a most respectable means by which historians attain their overriding goal: to find meaning in generalizations. The problem is that in the very act of producing the most reliable evidence for their conclusions, interpretation, thesis, or observations, they reduce to abstractions the people whose lives in past time they are seeking to explain. They thereby render them as faceless averages without particular identities and incapable of being described as actual human beings.

Once again, in all the major fields of historical study, and certainly in my own field of American history, examples abound. In such "statistical" studies, the evidence used throughout either was produced as statistical compilations or has been rendered statistical by the scholars themselves. The subjects of such studies are numerical abstractions; they do not become, in their author's hands, individualized human beings. Influential examples are Stephen Thernstrom's *Poverty and Progress: Social Mobility in a Nineteenth Century City*[5] and *The Other Bostonians: Poverty and Progress in the American Metropolis, 1880–1970*[6] and Peter Knights, *The Plain People of Boston, 1830–1860: A Study in City Growth.*[7]

In fairness, it should be added that many academic scholars, for a variety of reasons, have never been comfortable with statistical evidence and have not used it as the basis for their writings. Even those who at one time strongly believed in its efficacy, have since drawn back from basing whole studies on it. Perhaps such scholars have become sensitive to colleagues who have argued that statistical evidence is needlessly technical for what historians can actually learn from it and is abstract to the point that flesh and blood human beings are lost sight of. In any case, it has become far more typical for scholars to mix statistical and other kinds of evidence, and even those who accord a major place for statistics now typically mix such findings with anecdotal case studies of individualized human beings.

Nonetheless, whether or not particular scholars themselves use statistical evidence, academic historians as a group continue to hold statistical evidence in high esteem. The work of Thernstrom and Knights, cited above, has become very well known and influential. In each case, the authors used statistical evidence to validate their generalizations. All the human beings the authors had studied were rendered as abstractions, statistical groupings, rather than as actual individuals with identities, as persons capable of being described as individuals. Whenever other historians use statistical evidence in the course of their studies, the results are the same.

Title inflation and statistically based abstractions are two indications of an endemic tendency among academic historians to overgeneralize. The deeply felt need to find patterns of human behavior has led academic historians to seek ways of claiming omniscience in their understanding of their subject, even when they've only done research into bits of it. As a result, inflated titles and sweeping conclusions typically accompany a narrow source base. The generalizations historians make in their studies are often made respectable by statistically rendered evidence; this evidence reduces the people historians have studied into faceless, anonymous, identity-less abstractions.

Such is the great price paid by scholars who are deeply committed to conceptualizing, analyzing, interpreting, and synthesizing social reality. In their quest for meaningful generalizations, they have turned categorization into a new reality. But it cannot be made real. Categories remain what by nature they have to be: mental constructs. To rest our understanding of human life in social settings on such an enterprise is fraught with difficulty. This engrained Platonism has produced a certainty, a kind of arrogance among academic scholars that is quite unwarranted. The methods by which academics probe social reality yield insights, but they are always limited, tentative, and blatantly incomplete. Scholars should go forth in humility and not make excessive claims for what they are capable of adding to the pool of human wisdom.

Amateur historians, journalists, novelists, and storytellers are all natural empiricists, for all focus on particular individuals and particular circumstances and incidents. Their writings are vastly more popular than most academic writings, not simply because they dwell on real or imagined individuals and events, but because these writers instinctively realize that the only reality is what an individual can perceive as he or she lives out his or her life. From this perspective, concepts and models, interpretations and analyses and syntheses, statistical summations—all the ways of the academic mind—are inferior tools in the quest we all share for an understanding of human life. From the perspective of the journalist novelist storyteller amateur historian, particular individuals and particular incidents are what comprise human life, not the mind-play of concepts, models, and abstractions.

Humanistic scholars, especially historians, should pay attention to this nonacademic perspective. Academicians owe the larger public a much clearer explanation of what the aims and purposes of scholarship are. How seldom is such an effort made! Articulate spokesmen for academic studies are in a position to tell laypeople—in a language that they will understand—that scholars use methods and concepts and models in order to understand human life in a systematic way through analysis, synthesis, interpretation, and generalization. So much is obvious—from an academic standpoint. What these spokesmen should go on to say, however, is that this effort to reduce human life to comprehensible patterns adds to but does not replace the more ordinary way of understanding social reality.

What academic study adds—and it is something of great value, something that the lay public should be far more aware of than they ever have been—is an effort, at least, to understand objectively and scientifically, in a way that anyone who studies the same subject in the same manner would reach similar conclusions about what happened and why and what its consequences have been, and, finally, what it all means in its context. This has been a great effort, one of the greatest achievements of the human mind.

Academic study has also been terribly, inevitably limited in its capacity to extend our understanding of human life. Scholars need to declare the limitations of what they achieve much more emphatically than they ever have before. They need to be aware that what they offer the public supplements but does not replace concrete, descriptive accounts of life from an ordinary individual's standpoint. For, although scholars are individuals equipped with a special way of knowing, they are still individuals for all that.[8]

V

HISTORIANS AND COMMUNICATION

11

History as Writing

In Europe and North America, academic scholars are not usually accomplished writers. They do not receive any special training that would help them to become outstanding writers (or teachers, for that matter), even although as professors they are hired, given tenure, paid, and promoted on the basis of their published and therefore written scholarship, as well as on their ability to teach. Ironically, professors are trained primarily in how to do research in their particular disciplines and are initially hired because of a demonstrated capacity to do so. But even although their salary, tenure, and promotions are subsequently based on "publications" (and teaching performance), their lack of training in writing and the absence of any need for them to demonstrate unusual writing talent as a basis for their initial appointment or subsequent promotion means that scholars are rarely extraordinary writers. (I define such a writer to be anyone whose style attracts and holds the attention of readers beyond those who already have a developed interest in the writer's particular subject.)

I do not mean to imply that scholars are bad writers. They have to evaluate their students' writings on a continuing basis, just as they themselves have written essays, theses, and a dissertation, all of which were assessed in part as writings. All of their publications appear as some form of writing. But nothing in an academic career depends on the quality of a professor's writing. Although required to be literate, a scholar is not obliged to measure up to any more refined stylistic standards. Once again: This is because scholars are trained primarily to do research. The need to write out conclusions the scholar has derived from his or her research is a necessary part of the process of producing scholarship. But nowhere in the advanced study that historians and others undertake prior to their academic careers is there any formal testing of their capacity as writers. At no point thereafter is the unusual quality of the writing style the chief factor in determining whether a scholarly manuscript is accepted by a journal editor or a publisher for publication.

There is a serious problem with the current state of academic writing, as just sketched. Although academic scholars are trained to do research, and not to be writers (or teachers), it is widely recognized throughout the educational world that style and content are inseparable. That is, whatever one says is inseparable from how one says it. These two aspects of communication are as inextricably intertwined as the human mind and body. They can be analyzed separately, but what one person tries to communicate to others is best understood as a total reading experience in which something is conveyed well or badly, that is, clearly or confusedly, subtly or oversimply, fully or partially, convincingly or unconvincingly, memorably or forgettably, with sophistication or disingenuousness, in language that is apt and flows and allures or is inept and jerky or wooden and offputting.

If something is expressed verbally, it is meant to be listened to or read. It is in the act of listening or reading that the communicative contact is made. Writing is vastly different from the research and methodology that scholars are trained to focus on. Research and the method selected for conducting it involve the researchers and their material. By contrast, a piece of writing conveys information, opinions, observations, interpretations, and conclusions expressed by a particular individual (or group) as a form of communication to others. It is my contention that academic historians and scholars generally are capable, as writers, of conveying to a much wider readership than they have heretofore a great deal of significance about human life and the setting in which it exists. In order for this to happen, however, historians and other academics will have to examine carefully their role in society as writers and, by implication, reexamine the way they are trained.

In one sense, academic historians are not writers at all. In the West, during the twentieth century, true writers have been those whose principal occupation and income depend on the sale of their published work, in sharp contrast to the situation that exists for academic scholars. In a development whose origins lay in the seventeenth century, the increasingly varied writings of such writers appeared in an ever widening array of journals or newspapers, magazines, and books. However, before the twentieth century, writing of this kind was usually a partial occupation, shared with other pursuits and sources of income. Only during the nineteenth century, when journalism became a profession and when publishers arose to satisfy and shape the demand of a large, middle-class reading public, did printed writing sustain a sizable group of individuals financially and allow them to devote their adult lives to the act of writing. Such writers have never organized as a profession in the way that doctors, lawyers, or professors have, although a number of trade associations have emerged since the late nineteenth century.[1]

These professional writers continue to provide the lay reading public with fictional and factual accounts of all aspects of human life and its natural setting. Such writers are, with few exceptions, not academic scholars. The chief characteristic of their writing, regardless of its subject or of its factual or fictional mode, is its descriptive nature. Those who read these writings are either untrained in the academic way of examining or interpreting life or, even though exposed, do not usually seek, in their reading, accounts that force them to return to that kind of mental activity. The general reading public responds to vivid description, to fact and detail that create mental pictures, that awakens the sensory reactions of sight, sound, smell, taste, and feel. Writers who depend on this public have generally avoided abstractions and conceptualization.

During the eighteenth and nineteenth centuries, such writers typically produced both factual and fictional works, combining autobiography, biography, travel accounts, and social observation with poetry, plays, novels, and stories. "Literature" referred to everything these writers succeeded in having published. In this century, those whose principal occupation has been writing have tended to specialize in either fictional or factual kinds of writing.[2]

The terms *literature* and *writer* have come increasingly to refer to fiction and poetry and their creators. Writers of fiction—novelists, playwrights, and storytellers—have been generally accorded a place of higher esteem than other writers, those who have produced factual works. The equation of writing with fiction is a phenomenon in need of explanation. However, it is clear that the academic professorate has fostered this development, for Language and Literature departments in this century have increasingly focused on writings of a fictional and poetic character. Indeed, a host of academic and journalistic critics routinely links "writer" with fiction and provides voluminous analyses of such writings, leaving other kinds of writing without the same searching evaluation.

Why should professional writers of fiction and poetry receive more critical attention than writers who seek to understand humans and the world they live in on a factual basis? Why should academic critics in particular usually ignore academic writing as a form of writing? Where are the critical evaluations of historical, social, and physical scientific writing, as writing?

In fairness to those academic scholars who are engaged in "literary studies," why has there been such a marked tendency for the very best writers to concentrate on fictional or poetic writing? Why hasn't factually oriented writing usually been as important to them? Why should the most gifted writers concentrate on the creation of fiction or poetry or drama?

In any case, nonacademic historians, at least those who have also been accomplished writers, have favored depicting the past as a story, filled with factual plot, character, and setting—a true-life drama. Like fiction, history was about flesh and blood, individualized people acting out events that had a direction, that is, a beginning, a development, and an end. Many of these historians, especially local ones, have lacked the capacity to transform their material into stories, but the great national historians of the nineteenth and early twentieth centuries provided models for a fully developed historical form. (Undistinguished as writers, local historians have typically produced fact-laden accounts of their communities and of the leading families within them.) Nothing attests to the persistence of the "past-as-story" among the lay readership so convincingly as the continuous popularity of historical fiction.

In a parallel development, academic scholarship has emerged since the nineteenth century as a consequence of the specialization of knowledge.

"Professors" have studied human life and its setting in basically different ways from those favored by the "amateur" writers just identified. Academic scholars have become professionals and have developed arcane methods and procedures that require specialized and advanced training in order to be fully understood and appreciated. They have written journal articles and scholarly books in an increasingly technical and conceptual language, writing that usually evokes the interest of only those who have been similarly trained. To become an academic or professional, a person has to undergo rigorous, extended, and highly regulated study with an emphasis—as already indicated—on research and methodology. During the nineteenth and twentieth centuries, such scholars greatly added to the descriptive accounts that ordinary writers presented to the general reading public.[3]

In particular, academic historians have brought abstractions, conceptualization, theorizing, and model-making to historical writing. They have analyzed, synthesized, generalized, and interpreted people of all kinds in every aspect of their lives, utilizing anything perceived as evidence and employing a growing variety of methods and techniques. In the process, history as a story has been greatly altered, changed almost beyond recognition. During the twentieth century, historical scholarship has grown to mountainous proportions, as an ever increasing army of professors has written conference papers, journal articles, monographs, and studies.

But their writings are read by each other, or by their students, who constitute a large, captive audience for their work. Professors introduce university and college students to the academic mode of thinking in their lectures, discussions, and writings. Yet, typically, these students subsequently fail to show any sustained interest in academic scholarship—unless they become advanced students themselves. In other words, introducing substantial numbers of students to the academic mode of thinking has not produced a large and growing readership for academic scholarship.

The question is: Why? I believe that the answer is that the academic mode of thinking is difficult, and, unless committed to it, people—even those who have been involved in higher education—prefer the simpler, more direct, and immediate form of writing that "writers" have been presenting to the general reading public since the seventeenth century. Descriptive writing with vivid mental pictures involving one's sensory perceptions is a vastly more accessible way of communicating something in writing than is the abstract, conceptual, and technical manner of scholars. A major reason why the writing of academic historians has had such a limited readership is that it is presented by means of a difficult and complicated mode of thinking.

It can be argued that, in the hands of an effective, accomplished writer, such scholarship can awaken (and indeed has awakened) an interest in people beyond the academy. In every field of historical study, in every academic discipline, there are individual scholars who are gifted stylists, who have the capacity to synthesize or interpret in imaginative and bold ways. Their writings are reviewed in the book sections of major newspapers and magazines and are read by scholars and teachers and students in other disciplines as well as by the general public. Such individuals are extremely valuable to the entire academic enterprise. For the methods, procedures, evidence, and questions of historical and other forms of academic writing probe the nature of human life and its natural setting far more profoundly than descriptive accounts have done. It is therefore important that efforts be made to reach the widest possible readership.

What strikes me, however, is how few academic historians have successfully bridged the gap between the two contrasting kinds of historical writing just outlined, how few have mixed or amalgamated them effectively and attracted the lay public as well as students and colleagues. For while it is true that some in the academic world appreciate descriptive accounts of historical subjects, few readers outside of that world similarly appreciate academic writing.

During the twentieth century, popular and academic historical writings have increasingly appealed to two different and distinct groups of readers. Efforts to bridge the gap have been few and faltering. Is there not a serious danger to a civilization if its intellectual (or academic) elite gains knowledge in one way and the general public in another? Is there no way to try to unite the layperson and the specialist, the amateur and the professional, to make more widely accessible the heretofore arcane knowledge of the professorial elite? I think there is.

Academic scholars seek to find what is objectively true. This quest unites professors throughout the physical sciences, the social sciences, and the humanities. Each group does research and writes out its conclusions in an effort to articulate whatever will convince colleagues or fellow specialists that a true understanding of a subject has been attained. This deeply ingrained quest for objectivity—even with a growing awareness throughout the academic world of the irreducibly non-objective character of all human thinking—greatly and needlessly limits what scholars convey in their writings. What needs to be grasped much more firmly is that the highest objective of scholarship should be to understand human life and its setting, something that embraces objectivity but that also goes far beyond it.

An enhancement of our understanding of human life is at the core of the work of all the great nonacademic "writers" whose writings have circulated widely among the lay reading public. What these writers—poets, novelists, storytellers, playwrights, biographers, historians, philosophers, chroniclers, reporters, columnists, critics, and reviewers—have all been aware of is that insightful, memorable writing involves more than objective truth conveyed in prose written in an objective tone. They have all recognized the inextricable unity of what they say and how they say it, of content and style. More explicitly, they have appreciated the significance of selecting varied and apt tones as the vehicle through which to impart their understanding of their subject, and they have shown sensitivity and insight toward the multifarious qualities or characteristics of human life and consciousness that need to be explored and understood.

Surely, at the heart of any "classic," whether of a factual or fictional, a poetic or prosaic character, are memorable insights into the human condition. This is why people continue to read great books long after the circumstances that led to their creation have been forgotten. How else can an academic study attain this timelessness, become a classic, continue to be read well beyond the time it was produced, far from the time when a scholar's particular methodology prevailed? Is it the fate of most academic writing that it be "erased" or superceded by the work of the next generation of scholars, each confident that its methods are superior to those of all its predecessors?

The standard tone of academic writing is its objectivity—it should be distant, impersonal, measured, fair, even-handed. The writing doesn't call attention to itself. The writer is noninvolved, without any presence. The reader has little sense of what sort of a human being has written what he or she is reading. The objective tone presumes neutrality, absolute fairness. The impression created is that all aspects of the subject have been taken into account and given their just weight. The problem with academic writing presented in this tone is that it obscures a great deal of the process whereby inert historical materials are transmuted into a crafted historical interpretation. For even with methods and procedures for evaluating evidence and for interpreting whatever subject is being examined, historical investigation remains an enterprise characterized by a mixture of subjective and objective elements.

No two human beings will ever interpret particular historical evidence in exactly the same way, even when attempting to adhere to agreed-on methods of inquiry. Individual historians have their own varying views of human behavior, of human motivation and purpose, of human values and morality. In many ways these views shape the questions they ask, the focus they adopt, the evidence they give credence to. Historians are human beings of a certain age, gender, sexuality, socioeconomic class, and metaphysical/social/economic/political/cultural values or beliefs. In short, they are unique individuals, each with his or her distinctive profile and personality. All of these aspects of a particular historian's personal makeup influence how he or she perceives the past (as well as the present).

Therefore, an academic historian's writing would be greatly enriched if he or she would adopt varied tones in his or her writing, just as the best "writers" have always done. Such tones should most appropriately reflect his or her relationship to certain aspects of his or her subject, and would most effectively convey to readers either particular points or entire interpretations. These varied writing tones would not replace the objective "voice"; rather, they would augment it, make it more sophisticated, subtle, and nuanced. Readers would become aware that even the academic mode of thinking embraces a range of verbal expression that can evoke varied responses in them.

The objective voice serves to satisfy the reader's quest for objective truth, fact, information, and all that can be convincingly demonstrated to have happened. But this particular verbal tone leaves untouched a great range of possible mental/emotional/psychological reactions to writing that can deepen and enlarge the extent to which readers can attain an understanding of the subject being written about. Thus, academic thinking encased in writing with an objective tone greatly limits or impoverishes what academic historians are capable of conveying to a wide readership.

For example, scholars can also adopt a subjective tone in their writing. They can indicate in many different ways what their opinion of their subject is. By doing so, they can articulate what is there already: namely, that the act of trying to be objective, worthwhile and important as it is, always coexists with a personal attitude that the writer holds toward his subject. Why not make this attitude explicit, verbally precise? Does the writer admire or dislike his or her subject? Is he or she ambivalent or indifferent? Try as the writer does to be objective, his or her attitude will affect the selection of evidence and its evaluation as well as the emphasis placed on it.

Similarly, academic historians can also be critical and judgmental. They are perfectly capable of articulating in what ways, in their view, the people being studied measure up or fail to measure up to any standard historians have in mind—a standard they should also make explicit. Such historians are also capable of deploying other, ranging and varied verbal tones. There is no magic formula, no predetermined system of signals or cues for what should be selected. Some historians would do well, others badly or clumsily, but prevailing practice precludes most from even trying.

Such writers, either by turns or consistently, could be humorous, witty, satirical, sarcastic, mocking, condescending, irreverent, sorrowful, accusatory, condemnatory, laudatory, inspirational, earnest, playful, serious, lugubrious, empathetic, or sympathetic in tone. Once again: these word "voices"—or others like them—would not replace the objective tone. Instead, they would be added to it, for emphasis, to convey the author's feelings and insights and considered judgments, to evoke varied responses from readers in a way that engages the whole range of their emotions, their ethical sense, their beliefs and values, their psychological reactions, their intelligence and understanding.

In short, academic historians needlessly and harmfully seem imprisoned in one mode of writing. Academic research and study have produced a great deal of importance that should be conveyed to all who are literate, but academic historians communicate through an impoverished language. They (and other scholars) could communicate far more effectively than they do to the vast majority of readers who inhabit the world beyond the academy. Academic elites are capable of working to break down the barriers that separate their specialized, conceptualized, technical knowledge from the lay public. One major way is for them to extend and enlarge and enrich their language in the manner just sketched.

Scholars can use any well-known current critic, commentator, reviewer, essayist, or columnist as a model, or, from within their own ranks, the writings of widely read academics, such as John Kenneth Galbraith. Galbraith's interpretations of economic life have been enhanced by his instinctive understanding of the value that varied verbal tones have in academic writings nonetheless intended for a wide public. Similarly, from among the ranks of professional writers, Gore Vidal is a good example of one who employs varied verbal tones in his essays and reviews.

There is another, even more basic way that academic historians are failing to communicate with a large, literate public in the West. Quite properly, they have explored the past in an effort to explain how and why and when life evolved into its present forms and patterns. In this effort, they have greatly extended the historical knowledge of that small community that has actually read what they have written. But historical best-sellers remain books written in the popular mode, that is, descriptive accounts of people and events—vivid, dramatic, and highly sensitized to what is particular and unique.

Historical scholars cannot cease to be analytical, conceptual, and interpretive—all forms of intellectual activity endemic to the academic mode of thinking. But they can significantly extend the way they study the past and thus broaden the appeal of what they write. They can do what all great "writers" have done: they can examine the past for what it tells them about all the significant characteristics of human life. Thus, the study of history would become far richer and deeper than simply an explanation of how and why human life has evolved into what it is now, important as that is. Historical writing could take its place—once again—as one of several modes of inquiry that have as their objective an understanding of human life in all its important manifestations. I say "once again" because the view that history is "philosophy teaching by example" was the prevailing view of the more notable historians in Europe from the Renaissance to the eighteenth century.

In other words, academic historians could study a subject, not only to discover what happened and why and how life changed over time, but also to present whatever their study reveals about human life. In order to do this, however, scholars would have to learn a new vocabulary, a new historical "language." All that has actually happened in human life is a property of the past. All else is conjecture, prediction, imagination—or the fleeting present. There is no greater source—of a *factual* character—for observations on human life than history. Historians could greatly enrich their writings, and, without emasculating or attenuating their methods, they could significantly extend their effort to understand their subject.

By the nineteenth century, academic scholars moved historical inquiry away from the above concerns in an effort to be factual, truthful, and objective. Such efforts have enlarged our capacity to reconstruct the past and to extract what is significant and meaningful in it as an explanation for how life evolved into its present state. But these advances have been accompanied by a significant diminution in the historical enterprise as the burgeoning historical profession severed itself from a much older and deeper quest that great "writers" have always embarked upon—namely, the effort to understand human life itself.

I believe that the various characteristics of human life are best examined in clusters of related traits. For example, scholars have long paid attention to *irony* and *paradox* and *incongruities* in history, but they have tended to ignore the past's *congruities*, those things that "add up" and "make sense" together. Rarely do historians comment on either the *absurdity* or the *meaningfulness* of their subjects, although surely they must often be struck by one or the other. They frequently explore the *inevitability* of what they are studying, but much less often its *contingency*, or the unexpectedness of particular combinations of circumstances.

It is rare that a historian gives equal attention to both *change* and *continuity*, although both should command his attention. One cluster seems about equally well or badly handled: Historians sometimes find their subjects to be *contradictory* in their behavior and beliefs or values, but less often do they probe *ambivalence* as well. The *mood*, *attitude*, and *temperament* of people studied historically is sometimes focused on, as is the relative *simplicity* or *complexity* of their lives. Historians are less effective considering the matter of whether their subjects' lives are *obvious* or *incomprehensible* or even *mysterious*. Life tends to be "flattened out," to be turned into a question of whether there's enough evidence, and not something requiring the judgment of the historian.

Similarly, historians shy away from judging whether their subjects are *trivial, banal, sublime*, or *transcendent*—or whether they are (on the whole) *stupid, perverse*, or *intelligent*. Such scholars are often attracted to subjects that exhibit *willfulness* or *domination*, but less often to others displaying *passivity* or *submissiveness*. An engrained reluctance to serve as judges also means that historians don't test their subjects for degrees of *success* or *failure*, unless either is overwhelmingly obvious. The same is true of *disasters, calamities*, or just *irritations*, or—by contrast—*accomplishments*, or, to put it another way, *deprivations* or *fulfillments*.

Historians are particularly ineffectual in conveying the *tragedy, sadness, comedy*, or *humor* in their subjects; they shy away from considering the *pathos* or *bathos* in the human lives they've studied. These particular academic scholars are not usually effective in portraying such human emotions as *boredom, indifference, horror, terror, excitement, exhilaration*, or *sorrow, misery, suffering, joy, comfort, satisfaction*, or *pain* and *pleasure*. They are somewhat more effective—perhaps because the human record is more obvious—in writing about *cruelty, anger*, and *hate*, although less convincingly—perhaps because the opposite has been the case—in revealing *caring* and *love*. *Peacefulness* and *violence* are human states that historians have often focused on, although *avarice* and *sacrifice* or *arrogance, pride, honor, humility*, and *shame* have been far more difficult to convey.

Similarly, historians have little difficulty finding examples of human *constructiveness* and *cooperation* or, by contrast, *destructiveness* and *competition*, but traits such as *crudity* and *gracefulness* are rarely considered. Nor do scholars often probe together indications of *normality, insanity, neurosis*, or *psychosis* in their subjects. Even degrees of *integrity* or *hypocrisy* are rarely explored. And, once again, because of an extreme reluctance to pass judgment, there is rarely much comment on the *sanctity, goodness*, and *virtue* or *badness, evil*, or *vice* of the people under investigation.

These italicized terms are what I mean by the basic characteristics of human life. Notice that I am not suggesting that historians presently ignore them altogether, but rather that such scholars are not trained to make them a central concern of their research and writing. Whenever human characteristics like these are actually made germane to academic scholarship, it means that particular historians have somehow significantly gone beyond their training and enlarged their perception of what writing history encompasses.

Once again: The past provides us with our factual basis for making observations and judgments about human life; the present is too fleeting for considered assessments. Historians are therefore in the best position to interpret what being human has actually meant. The importance of historical writing could become greatly enhanced if academic scholars would augment their questions and methods, their analyses and interpretations, with probings of the human condition through examination of such characteristics as those just enumerated.

There are no simple formulas for this vastly important undertaking, just as there aren't any for the adoption of varied and appropriate verbal tones and voices. If explorations of timeless, pertinent characteristics of human life were to become as ordinary a part of such writing as the quest to reconstruct the past and to explain how and why and when it evolved over time into what it now is, then doubtless some historians would fare well at their new task and others would not.

But if scholars are even to attempt to establish a common basis for communicating with all those who want to read about the past, they are going to have to do what all great writers have always done—probe the human condition. They would not have to popularize what they do, that is, transmute their findings into wholly descriptive accounts. They would not have to relinquish what it means to think academically, to conceptualize, interpret, analyze, synthesize, and generalize—although far greater efforts should be made to define terms and otherwise make abstractions concrete and vivid and precise for readers unused to thinking in such ways. They wouldn't even have to alter their technically sophisticated methodologies, although much closer attention should be paid to how clearly such methods are explained to people who, unlike colleagues, are utterly unfamiliar with them.   What *is* needed is for scholars to have both a well-developed appreciation of the overall nature of human life and a much-tested capacity to comment in varied verbal tones on whatever characteristics seem present in the subject they've studied.

In this way, academic historians could make a significant move toward reintegrating of elitist and popular ways of understanding the past, and grope their way toward a new common ground for both the lay public and the academic elite. Such a ground existed before the swift emergence of professional historians during the nineteenth and twentieth centuries. These historians already have much of importance to say about the human past, but their capacity to communicate to the larger, general reading public is unnecessarily restricted. By probing the human condition, they could attract the attention of that larger public by doing what all great writers have always done. After all, human beings of all intellectual levels turn to the joke, the anecdote, the tale, and myth for explanations of what it means to be human.   Why should historical and other forms of academic writing be separated from this quest?

In order for historical scholars, as a group, to do in a collective and routine way what I've suggested here, they would have to alter significantly the structure of their graduate study to include courses on writing and teaching. They would have to perceive their craft in a vastly different way. Above all else, they would have to see themselves as writers and history, not as a research project, but as writing.

Notes

CHAPTER 2

1. Two examples that come readily to my mind are the Puritans of colonial New England, who instituted direct democracy for white male voters, and the colonial Virginians, who developed a local form of "republicanism" based on a relatively close-knit white population who also created the most comprehensive system of human slavery ever known. Both groups were notably "democratic" among themselves, but profoundly conservative with respect to "outsiders" of any kind.

CHAPTER 4

1. I am referring here only to fully developed forms of nationalism, linked, as they have been, to modern nation-states. Boyd Shafer, in his extensive studies of the phenomenon, carefully distinguishes between mature nationalism and earlier, nascent forms that developed in Europe before the eighteenth century. Boyd Shafer, *Nationalism: Myth and Reality* (New York: Harcourt, Brace, and World, 1955) and *Faces of Nationalism* (New York: Harcourt, Brace, and World, 1972). The academic study of nations and nationalism has been a twentieth-century phenomenon, and the scholarship has burgeoned since the 1960s. Recent treatments are Eric Hobsbawm's *Nations and Nationalism Since 1780: Programme, Myth, Reality* (Cambridge, England: Cambridge University Press, 1990), an account that is focused on Europe, and Liah Greenfeld, *Nationalism: Five Roads to Modernity* (Cambridge, Mass.: Harvard University Press, 1992), which focuses on Britain, France, Germany, Russia, and the United States. The most influential essay has been David M. Potter, "The Historian's Use of Nationalism and Vice-Versa," *American Historical Review* 67 (1962): 924–950. The most influential book-length study has probably been Benedict Anderson, *Imagined Communities: Reflections on the Origins and Spread of Nationalism* (London: Verso, 1983).

2. The role of the American nation in formalizing this global system has been of crucial importance, given the leading role of Presidents Woodrow Wilson (in the case of the League of Nations), Franklin Roosevelt, and Harry Truman (in the case of the United Nations).

3. On Japan see Delmar Myers Brown, *Nationalism in Japan: An Introductory Historical Analysis* (New York: Russell and Russell, reprint 1977 (1955)). Although they had for centuries possessed some of the hallmarks of nationalism, such as geographic isolation and ethnic/religious/linguistic unity, it wasn't until the restored empire became susceptible to Western influences that the Japanese created a modern nation—and became nationalistic. In the first half of the twentieth century, the Japanese Empire also mirrored European empires by becoming imperialistic and colonialistic in Asia. On China see Krishnalal Chatterli, *The National Movement in Modern China* (Calcutta: F.K.L. Mukhopadhyay, 1958).

4. Some independent political entities in Asia were never colonialized by the Europeans, or were colonized by fellow Asians, particularly the Japanese and the Chinese: such nations as Iran, Afghanistan, Korea, Manchuria, Mongolia, and Tibet.

5. Some scholars argue that, in the twentieth century, the Soviet Union was and China continues to be an "empire" even though neither national government "colonized" in the classic sense of adding politically subservient colonial territories. Both governments incorporated territory, adding it to the nation, in the same way that in the nineteenth century the American government added territories that it later admitted to the union as equal states. At this point, the question is legitimately raised: Has the United States, therefore, also been an "empire"?

6. Hobsbawm's *Nations and Nationalism* is filled with instances of such exaggeration and distortion within Europe.

7. Greenfeld, *Nationalism: Five Roads to Modernity,* for Europe as a whole. For Britain in particular see Linda Colley, *Britons: Forging the Nation, 1707–1837* (New Haven, Conn.: Yale University Press, 1992).

8. Anderson, *Imagined Communities.*

9. R.S. Chavan, *Nationalism in Asia* (New Delhi: Sterling Publishers, 1973) is a good supplement to Anderson's *Imagined Communities.*

10. Indeed, Boyd Shafer argues that the emergence of nationalism as the most potent of modern abstractions and of the nation-state as the entity to which its citizens give their supreme loyalty must be understood as a slow, evolutionary process under which individuals and groups gave up close and important forms of identification with lesser corporate bodies—particular churches, guilds, unions, fraternal and maternal associations, local communities, and various forms of feudalistic arrangements—over decades and centuries in an enormously complicated, variegated way across the globe. See Shafer, *Nationalism: Myth and Reality* and *Faces of Nationalism: New Realities and Old Myths.*

11. William H. McNeill's *Polyethnicity and National Unity in World History* (Toronto, Ontario: University of Toronto Press, 1986) is instructive on this point. Anthony D. Smith, in *The Ethnic Origins of Nations* (London: Basil Blackwell, 1986), argues that, throughout human history, ethnic groups have exhibited the same kind of identity as modern national groups. Both have relied on common myths and symbols and have shared historical experiences as the basis for their unity and distinctiveness.

12. The emergence of capitalism as an expansionist economic system has been most notably studied in the work of Immanuel Wallerstein, *The Modern World-System,* 3 vols. (New York: Academic Press, 1974–1988) and Fernand Braudel, *Civilization and Capitalism: 15th–18th Centuries* 3 vols. (New York: Harper and Row, 1981–1984).

13. Similarly, before the modern era, people had for many centuries exhibited forms of identification and loyalty that were both intensely localized and as wide as such ancient civilizations as the Mesopotamian, Egyptian, Hellenistic, Indian, and Chinese, or such medieval civilizations as Christian Europe and the Islamic world. But there is no more evidence from the premodern era than there is from modern times that the nonpolitical aspects of life were neatly contained within political boundaries.

14. The most significant studies of American nationalism are Merle Curti, *The Roots of American Loyalty* (New York: Columbia University Press, 1946), Hans Kohn, *American Nationalism: An Interpretive Essay* (New York: Macmillan Co., 1957), Paul Nagel, *One Nation Indivisible: The Place of the Union in American Thought* (New York: Oxford University Press, 1966), and *This Sacred Trust: American Nationality, 1798–1898* (New York: Oxford University Press, 1971), and, most recently, Wilbur Zelinsky, *Nation into State: The Shifting Symbolic Foundations of American Nationalism* (Chapel Hill: University of North Carolina Press, 1988).

15. Daniel J. Boorstin, *The Americans: The National Experience* (New York: Random House, 1965), pp. 373–390.

16. This was David Potter's main point in his "The Historian's Use of Nationalism and Vice-Versa." In his view, the American Civil War occurred because Southerners were unable, in 1860–1861, to sustain their multiple allegiances in a harmonious, complementary way.

17. Zelinsky, in *Nation into State*, demonstrates that American nationalism had a very broad foundation; it embodied the notion that Americans were embarked on a unique enterprise. But, increasingly, especially by the late nineteenth century, nationalist sentiment was focused on the state itself: the purpose of nationalist fervor was the glorification of the national government and its instrumentalities. This tight association between nationalism and the state mirrors developments in Europe. See Hobsbawm, *Nations and Nationalism*, pp. 80–100.

18. Dorothy Ross, in *The Origins of American Social Science* (Cambridge, England: University of Cambridge Press, 1991), shows that this predilection was in evidence from the very origins of the various social sciences as academic disciplines in the United States.

19. Ian Tyrrell, in "American Exceptionalism in an Age of International History," *American History Review*, 96, no. 4 (October 1991), 1038–1043, makes a similar point about the inability of historians of the United States to "bind" their territory to any larger unit.

20. (New York: Basic Books, 1963). See *Continental Divide: The Institutions and Values of the United States and Canada* (New York: Routledge, 1990).

21. (Oxford: Clarendon Press, 1991) The papers were focused on government policy, economic development, religion, education, culture, and society. The participants were Seymour Martin Lipset, Daniel Bell, Peter Temin, Andrew M. Greeley, Aaron Wildavsky, Martin Trow, Richard Rose,and Byron E. Shafer.

22. Shafer, "What Is the American Way? Four Themes in Search of Their Next Incarnation," in *Is America Different?*, pp. 222–261.

23. Martin Trow, "American Higher Education: 'Exceptional' or Just Different," in Shafer, *Is America Different?*, pp. 138–186. (Shafer's summary: p. 253.)

24. Peter Temin, "Free Land and Federalism: American Economic Exceptionalism," in Shafer, ed., *Is America Different?*, pp. 71–93.

25. *American Historical Review* 96, no. 4 (October 1991): 1044–1053.

CHAPTER 5

1. For example, in *Families and Communities: A New View of American History* (Nashville, Tenn.: American Association for State and Local History, 1974), I attempted to organize American history on the basis of levels of community—everything from families to localities, to states and regions, to the nation itself. I contended that the nation was not the primary context for people living within its borders until the twentieth century. Similarly, Robert Wiebe, in *The Segmented Society* (New York: Oxford University Press, 1975), presented an America that has been persistently characterized by its segmented character—that is, its divisions into multifarious groups.

More recently, Thomas Bender, in "Wholes and Parts: The Need for Synthesis in American History" (*Journal of American History*, 73, no. 1, [June 1986]: 120-136), proposed that political history be redefined as "public culture" or "power in public": "With such a sense of public culture, we approach the complex intermingling at once contested and collaborative, of political, economic, social, and cultural life" (126). In particular, Bender urged that the much-studied social groupings be examined in a public as well as a private context, in order to show how they shared or contested power and influence. Bender thus attempted to combine political and social history in a new synthesis involving parts and wholes.

2. This fundamental fact of American political life greatly limits the workability of any proposed synthesis (such as Thomas Bender's) which would connect the history of social groups with the activities of the U.S. government or, more broadly, to public life in America.

3. The expansion of governmental activity since the eighteenth century has been a global phenomenon. I do not mean to imply that political "cultures" haven't, at certain times and places, been organizing mechanisms of great authority in the lives of particular groups of citizens. Through the human past, there have been political systems of remarkable durability and power. The most spectacular example is that of Imperial China, a centralized bureaucracy committed to a particular philosophy (Confucianism) that governed a large empire for many centuries. A more modern example is the English (and then British) governmental system, both nationally and, since around 1600, internationally.

4. In my view, American colonial history is even more difficult to study in a satisfactory and meaningful way, because it lacks even the natural political boundaries that the United States has provided since 1776. In recent decades, scholars of the colonial period have usually ignored the "imperial" perspective that guided the work of an earlier generation and have tended to impose a kind of retrospective unity on the colonies in which rebellion occurred, making them a proto-nation. But the fact remains that the only natural political context for studying these colonies is to deal with them as parts of a larger entity, namely, the British Empire.

In *Albion's Seed: Four British Folkways in America* (New York: Oxford University Press, 1989), David Hackett Fischer has embarked on a multivolume "cultural history of the United States" (in the anthropological and not the aesthetic sense), based on four persisting regional "folkways." Fischer finds evidence for regional variations for many significant aspects of life during the early colonial period, for such things as speech, building, family, marriage, gender, sexuality, child-rearing, naming, age, death, religion, magic, learning, food, dress, sport, work, time, wealth, rank, association, order, power, and freedom. But, in my view, there will be a basic problem in organizing subsequent volumes on the basis of the persistence of the four regional "cultures" that Fischer has found were present at the outset of British settlement in North America. The problem stems from the fact that these folkways became less important as time went on. Fischer's scheme substitutes a rigid regionalism for a similarly distorted nationalism as another procrustean bed on which to fit all of the American past. Regionalism is a no more satisfactory organizing principle than nationalism has been, in spite of efforts stretching back to the work of Frederick Jackson Turner early in this century.

A similar effort by an historical geographer is D. W. Meinig, *The Shaping of America: A Geographical Perspective on 500 Years of History*, Vol. 1, *Atlantic America, 1492–1800* (New Haven, Conn.: Yale University Press, 1986). Both Fischer and Meinig have returned to the earlier trans-Atlantic or "imperial" perspective.

5. Well-known accounts of particular aspects of family life, such as Oscar and Mary Handlin's *Facing Life: Youth and the Family in American History* (Boston: Little, Brown, 1971), Joseph Kett's *Rites of Passage: Adolescence in America, 1790 to the Present* (New York: Basic Books, 1977), Carl Degler's *At Odds: Women and the Family in America from the Revolution to the Present* (New York: Oxford University Press, 1980), David Hackett Fischer's *Growing Old in America* (New York: Oxford University Press, 1977), W. Andrew Achenbaum's *Old Age in the New Land: The American Experience Since 1790* (Baltimore Md: Johns Hopkins University Press, 1978), and Carole Haber's *Beyond Sixty Five: The Dilemma of Old Age in America's Past* (Cambridge, England: Cambridge University Press, 1983)—all share a "national" definition.

6. *Four Generations: Population, Land, and Family in Colonial Andover, Massachusetts* (Ithaca, N.Y.: Cornell University Press, 1970), pp. 261–289.

7. For example, a recent survey of U.S. urban history by Eric Monkkonen, *America Becomes Urban: The Development of U.S. Cities and Towns, 1780–1980* (Berkeley: University of California Press, 1988) , while it briefly connects U.S. cities to the history of cities generally and everywhere, quickly goes on to focus on urban development within the United States.

8. *A New England Town/The First Hundred Years: Dedham, Massachusetts, 1636–1736* (New York: W. W. Norton, 1970), pp. 18–22.

9. The best known studies of this kind are: Frank Tannenbaum, *Slave and Citizen: The Negro in the Americas* (New York: Knopf, 1947); Stanley Elkins, *Slavery: A Problem in American Intellectual and Institutional Life* (Chicago: University of Chicago Press, 1959); David Brion Davis, *The Problem of Slavery in Western Culture* (Ithaca, N.Y.: Cornell University Press, 1966) and *The Problem of Slavery in the Age of Revolution, 1770–1823* (Ithaca, N.Y.: Cornell University Press, 1975); and, most recently, Robert Fogel, *Without Consent or Contract: The Rise and Fall of American Slavery* (New York: W. W. Norton, 1989).

10. George Frederickson, *White Supremacy: A Comparative Study in American and South African Slavery* (New York: Oxford University Press, 1981). Comparisons of other kinds are also illuminating. For example see Peter Kolchin, *Unfree Labor: American Slavery and Russian Serfdom* (Cambridge, Mass.: Harvard University Press, 1987).

11. For example, neither Gerda Lerner's essays on the nature of women's history (*The Majority Finds Its Past: Placing Women in History* {New York: Oxford University Press, 1979}) nor such standard accounts of the subject as Page Smith's *Daughters of the Promised Land: Women in American History* (Boston: Little, Brown, 1970) and Mary P. Ryan's *Womanhood in America: From Colonial Times to the Present* (New York: New Viewpoints,

1975) go beyond the American or national perspective. But some historians who have studied women's history, especially feminism, have probed wider perspectives: for example, Richard J. Evans, *The Feminists: Women's Emancipation Movements in Europe, America, and Australasia* (London: Croom Helm, and New York: Barnes and Noble, 1977) and Jane Rendall, *The Origins of Modern Feminism: Women in Britain, France, and the United States, 1780–1860* (London: Macmillan Education, 1985).

12. For example, John Bodnar in his *The Transplanted: A History of Immigrants in Urban America* (Bloomington Indiana University Press, 1985) devotes only one-fourth of his study to the European phase, which is presented as background for the main subject. Similarly, David Hackett Fischer's *Albion's Seed: Four British Folkways in America* (New York: Oxford University Press, 1989), which focuses on the migrations from Britain to its North American colonies, deals with the British background for each of four regional migratory groups in one-quarter of the total space devoted to each group. By contrast, Gary Nash dealt with the cultural and social interchanges among natives, slaves, Africans, and various groups of European migrants within the context of the entire trans-Atlantic world in his *Red, White, and Black: The Peoples of Early America* (Englewood Cliffs, N.J.: Prentice-Hall, 1974), which, in my view, is what scholars of immigration should routinely do.

13. On the middle class see Stuart M. Blumin, *The Emergence of the Middle Class: Social Experience in the American City, 1760–1900* (Cambridge, England: Cambridge University Press, 1989).

On the rich see Edward Pessen's *Riches, Class, and Power Before the Civil War* (Lexington, Mass.: D.C. Heath, 1973) [a study focused on Boston, New York, including Brooklyn, and Philadelphia] and E. Digby Baltzell's *Philadelphia Gentlemen: The Making of a National Upper Class* (Glencoe, Ill.: Free Press, 1958) and *Puritan Boston and Quaker Philadelphia: Two Protestant Elites and the Spirit of Class Authority and Leadership* (New York: Free Press, 1979), and, more recently, Robert F. Dalzell's *Enterprising Elite: The Boston Associates and the World They Made* (Cambridge, Mass.: Harvard University Press, 1987).

On the laboring or working classes: Alan Dawley, *Class and Community: The Industrial Revolution in Lynn* (Cambridge, Mass.: Harvard University Press, 1976) and Sean Wilentz, *Chants Democratic: New York City and the Rise of the American Working Class, 1788–1850* (New York: Oxford University Press, 1984).

14. General accounts of religious history, such as Sidney Ahlstrom's *A Religious History of the American People* (New Haven, Conn.: Yale University Press, 1972) and, more recently, George Marsden's *Religion and American Culture* (New York: Harcourt Brace Jovanovich, 1990) and Jon Butler's *Awash in a Sea of Faith: Christianizing the American People* (Cambridge, Mass.: Harvard University Press, 1990) are almost entirely focused on religion within the United States.

Similarly, surveys of American economic history, such as Stuart Bruchey's recent *The Wealth of a Nation: An Economic History of the United States* (New York: Harper and Row, 1989) have not gone beyond a national perspective.

15. For example, such recent studies of medicine and science as Paul Starr's *The Social Transformation of American Medicine* (New York: Basic Books, 1982), Charles E. Rosenberg's *The Care of Strangers: The Rise of America's Hospital System* (New York: Basic Books, 1987), and Daniel J. Kevles, *The Physicists: The History of a Scientific Community in Modern America* (New York: Knopf, 1987) are all national in scope.

16. For example, Allen Guttmann's *A Whole New Ball Game: An Interpretation of American Sports* (Chapel Hill University of North Carolina Press, 1988) is confined to a consideration of sports in the United States, even though Guttmann draws on his own earlier, transnational inquiry into the nature of sport: *From Ritual to Record: The Nature of Modern Sports* (New York: Columbia University Press, 1978).

17. Studies as broadly integrative and interpretive as Lawrence W. Levine's *Highbrow/Lowbrow: The Emergence of a Cultural Hierarchy in America* (Cambridge, Massachusetts: Harvard University Press, 1988) and Alan Trachtenberg's *The Incorporation of America: Culture and Society in the Gilded Age* (New York: Hill and Wang, 1982) are still thoroughly nationalistic in their coverage. Neil Harris's *The Artist in American Society: The Formative Years, 1790–1860* (Chicago: University of Chicago Press, 1966) and Barbara Novak's *Nature and Culture: American Landscape and Painting, 1825–1875* (New York: Oxford University Press, 1980) both focus on American art and artists, but, in a portion of their studies, at least, they deal with European influences on that art and those artists. Novak's Chapter Ten, "America and Europe: Influence and Affinity," is an especially well-focused effort.

18. Surveys from Merle Curti's *The Growth of American Thought* (New York: Harper and Row, 1943) to Lewis Perry's *Intellectual Life in America: A History* (Chicago: University of Chicago Press, 1984) have been confined to a national perspective. Even more specific studies, those, for instance, on the impact of the European Enlightenment in America, are focused almost entirely on North America, not Europe: Henry F. May, *The Enlightenment in America* (New York: Oxford University Press, 1976) and Henry Steele Commager, *The Empire of Reason: How Europe Imagined and America Realized the Enlightenment* (New York: Oxford University Press, 1977).

19. David Hollinger has asked intellectual historians in particular to be clear as to whether they are dealing with distinctly "American" thought or with "thought in America." He has suggested that they examine what Americans as Americans have propounded of a philosophical character. (David Hollinger, "American Intellectual History: Issues for the 1980's," in Stanley I Kutler and Stanley N. Katz, eds., *The Promise of American History: Progress and Prospects* [Baltimore Md.: Johns Hopkins University Press, 1982], pp. 306–317.) But, in my view, these distinctions are not useful ones. The thought of Americans has not usually been determined by the degree to which Americans have been self-consciously "American" at the time any given ideas have been advocated. The only exception to this has been in the case of political philosophy, when ideas have been applied to a population organized politically in a nation-state. In this realm of thought, Americans have been defined by their citizenship, and Americans as a group have been perceived as a political entity.

20. A recent summary of academic writings on the American character is contained in Rupert Wilkinson, *The Pursuit of American Character* (New York: Harper and Row, 1988). All such efforts—including Wilkinson's own—are, in my judgment, foredoomed to failure because they involve gross overgeneralization. They all assume a unity in the behavior of the inhabitants of the United States that is simply not there.

21. For example, Daniel Levine, *Poverty and Society: The Growth of the American Welfare State in International Comparison* (New Brunswick, N.J.: Rutgers University Press, 1988). The nations compared are Britain, Germany, Denmark, and the United States.

22. For example, a pioneering collection of essays on this subject focused on the United States and other nation-states as the basis for comparisons, and not geographic territories of varied definitions. See C. Vann Woodward, ed., *The Comparative Approach to American*

History (New York: Basic Books, 1968).

23. The three "levels" of time that Fernand Braudel favored—the event (the short term), the conjuncture (the middle term or cycles), and the longue duree (the long term or structures)—were offered as suggestions, not as prescriptions. Synthesizers would do well to adapt them to the particular configurations of the American past. I believe that each aspect of American life—political, economic, social, cultural-intellectual—ought to be presented with reference to all three of these categories. For example, it is a mistake to link geography only to structure, economic development only to conjuncture, and politics only to events, I would argue. The best summary reference to Braudel's terms is in Fernand Braudel, *On History* (Chicago: University of Chicago Press, 1980), 74–75.

24. For further evidence that scholars have begun to question the notion that the national perspective is the most revealing from which to study the past, see Ian Tyrrell, "American Exceptionalism in an Age of International History," *American Historical Review* 96, no. 4 (October 1991): 1031–1055.

CHAPTER 6

1. The best overall account of Turner's career and writings is Richard Hofstadter, *The Progressive Historians: Turner, Beard, and Parrington* (New York: Knopf, 1968), pp. 47–164.

2. Arthur M. Schlesinger, Sr., "The City in American Civilization," in *Paths to the Present* (New York: Macmillan, 1949), pp. 210–235. For an early critique of Schlesinger's thesis, a critique that focused on a perceived ambiguity in such terms as city, urban, and urbanization, see William Diamond, "On the Dangers of an Urban Interpretation of History," in Eric Goldman, ed., *Historiography and Urbanization* (Baltimore Md.: Johns Hopkins University Press, 1941), pp. 67–108.

3. Eric E. Lampard, "American Historians and the Study of Urbanization," *American Historical Review* 65, (October 1961): 49–61.

4. Theories of urbanization that became well known appeared in Adna Weber, *The Growth of the City in the Nineteenth Century: A Study in Statistics* (New York: Macmillan 1899), in studies done by Roger Park and his associates at the University of Chicago (the "Chicago school") during the 1920s; in Louis Wirth, "Urbanism as a Way of Life," *American Journal of Sociology*, 44 (July, 1938): 1–24; in Herbert J. Gans, "Urbanism and Suburbanism as Ways of Life: A Re-Evaluation of Definitions," in Arnold Rose, ed., *Human Behavior and Social Processes* (Boston: Houghton Mifflin, 1962); in Leo F. Schnore, "The City as a Social Organism," *Urban Affairs Quarterly* 1 no. 3, (March 1966): 58–69.

5. Lampard, "American Historians and the Study of Urbanization."

6. Roy Lubove, "The Urbanization Process: An Approach to Historical Research," *Journal of the American Institute of Planners* 33 (January 1967), 33–39.

7. Philip Olson, "Rural American Community Studies: The Survival of Political Ideology," *Human Organization* 64, no. 4 (1964): 342–350. The history of rural sociology has rather often been traced, at least in inquiries of journal-article length: see Charles J. Galpin, "The Development of the Science and Philosophy of American Rural Society," *Agricultural History* 12, (July 1938): 195–208, Gilbert Fite, "Expanded Frontiers in Agricultural History," *Agricultural History* 35 (October 1961), 175–181; Harold T. Pinkett, "Government Research Concerning Problems of American Rural Society," *Agricultural History*, 58, no. 3 (1984): 365–372; Harry C. McDean, "Professionalism in the Rural Social Sciences, 1896–1919," *Agricultural History*, 58, no. 3 (1984): 373–392. Especially useful

is the article by Pinkett.

8. For a study of only one such agency sponsored by the Department of Agriculture, the Wisconsin Agricultural Experiment Station, see John H. Kolb, *Emerging Rural Communities: Group Relations in Rural Society/A Review of Wisconsin Research in Action* (Madison: University of Wisconsin Press, 1959).

9. Rural sociologists seem to have belatedly become alarmed by their collective failure to develop a respectable body of theory. I say "belatedly" because in the pages of their main journal, *Rural Sociology*, there seems to have been a rush of journal articles addressing the problem, but only after rural society had presumably declined to the point that its continued existence was in some doubt. See Gene F. Summers, Lawrence H. Seiler, and John P. Clark, "The Renewal of Community Sociology," *Rural Sociology* 35 (June, 1970): 218–231; J. Steven Picou and others, "Paradigms, Theories, and Methods in Contemporary Rural Sociology," *Rural Sociology* 43, no. 4 (1978): 559–583; Michael K. Miller, and Albert E. Luloff, "Who Is Rural? A Topological Approach to the Examination of Rurality," *Rural Sociology* 46, no. 4 (1981): 608–625; William H. Friedland, "The End of Rural Society and the Future of Rural Sociology," *Rural Sociology* 47, no. 4 (1982): 589–608 . See also: Peter H. Argersinger, "The People's Past: Teaching American Rural History," *History Teacher* 10 (May 1977): 403–424. Those who have sought to define rural history in the light of the obvious urban dominance of the mid-twentieth century include Neal Gross,"Sociological Variation in Contemporary Rural Life," *Rural Sociology* 13 (1948): 256–269; W. Keith Warner, "Rural Society in a Post-Industrial Age," *Rural Sociology* 39, no. 3 (1974): 306–318; Fred E.H. Schroeder, "Types of American Small Towns and How to Read Them," *Southern Quarterly* 19, no. 1 (1980): 104–135.

10. This was the case whether the inquiry concerned the overall history of rural life, as in the case of Robert Swierenga, in "The New Rural History: Defining the Parameters," *Great Plains Quarterly* 1, no. 4 (1981): 211–223 and "Theoretical Perspectives on the New Rural History: From Environmentalism to Modernization," *Agricultural History* 56, no. 3 (1982): 495–502, or whether the inquiry concerned a particular period of U.S. history, as in the case of Darret B. Rutman on colonial America, in "Assessing the Little Communities of Early America," *William and Mary Quarterly* 43, no. 2 (1986): 163–178, and as in the case of Russell B. Nye in "Changes in Twentieth Century Rural Society," *Midcontinent American Studies Journal* 10, no. 1 (1969) 25–40.

11. For example, Robert Redfield, *The Little Community* (Chicago: University of Chicago Press, 1956), p. 117.

12. This is certainly the case in Roland L. Warren's influential study of community, *The Community in America* (Chicago: Rand McNally, 1963).

13. George A. Hillery, Jr., "Definitions of Community: Areas of Agreement." *Rural Sociology* 20 (1955): 111–123; the quotation is from page 111.

14. Harold F. Kaufman, "Toward an Interactional Conception of Community," *Social Forces* 38 (1959): 8–17.

15. Albert J. Reiss, Jr., "The Sociological Study of Communities," *Rural Sociology* 24 (1959): 118–130.

16. Willis A. Sutton, Jr., and Jiri Kolaja, "The Concept of Community," *Rural Sociology* 25 (1960): 197–203.

17. (Chicago: Rand McNally, 1963).

18. *Rural Sociology* 30 (1965): 127–149.

19. Redfield, *The Little Community*. Anthropologists, unlike sociologists, had already devised a scheme of "levels" of community, from the smallest to those with vast territoriality.

20. Conrad M. Arensberg, "American Communities," *American Anthropologist* 57 (1955): 1143–1162.

21. Conrad M. Arensberg, "The Community as Object and as Sample," *American Anthropologist* 63, no. 2, part 1 (1961): 241–264.

CHAPTER 7

1. *Commercial Atlas and Marketing Guide* (Chicago: Rand McNally, any year).

2. Daniel J. Boorstin, *The Americans: The Democratic Experience* (New York: Random House, 1973), pp. 1–103.

3. For an effective brief account see John Stilgoe, *Common Landscape of America, 1580 to 1845* (New Haven, Conn.: Yale University Press, 1982), pp. 99–107.

4. Page Smith, *As a City upon a Hill: The Town in American History* (New York: Knopf, 1966), pp. 30–36.

5. Richard Lingeman, *Small Town America: A Narrative History* (New York: G.P. Putnam's, 1980), pp. 444–450.

6. See Kevin Lynch, *The Image of the City* (Cambridge, Mass.: M.I.T. Press, 1960).

7. Stillgoe, *Common Landscape of America*, pp. 18–19.

8. Smith, *As a City upon a Hill: The Town in American History* (New York: Knopf, 1966), pp. 214–217.

9. Fernand Braudel provided a definition for local place communities in *The Identity of France*: Volume One—*History and Environment* (New York: Harper and Row, 1988), pp. 139–146, 162–166, 180–189. But his scheme—which includes hamlets, villages, bourgs, and towns (which are seen as urban centers)—embraces France, not the world, although scholars of such communities in Britain have similarly linked towns to urban life. By contrast, local historians in the United States have not so unambiguously regarded towns as urban. Towns have usually occupied the place Braudel reserves for bourgs. My own view is that local place communities need to be seen as occupying various positions along a spectrum or continuum, whatever terminology one uses or whatever categories one establishes. The categories of "small" community and "large" community, whatever they are called, are always dependent on a context provided by time and place.

CHAPTER 8

1. Lingeman, *Small Town America,* p. 321.

2. The best overall account is in Daniel J. Boorstin, *The Americans: The National Experience* (New York: Random House, 1965), pp. 65–90.

3. For a good brief account, see Stilgoe, *Common Landscape of America,* pp. 231–238.

4. The best overall account is in Boorstin, *The Americans: The Democratic Experience* (New York: Random House, 1973), pp. 165–244.

5. A more restricted definition—the "consumption community"—is given in Boorstin, *The Americans: The Democratic Experience*, pp. 89–164.

CHAPTER 10

1. (Cambridge, Mass.: Harvard University Press, 1976).
2. (Albany, N.Y.: State University of New York Press, 1981).
3. (New York: Columbia University Press, 1979).
4. (Urbana: University of Illinois Press, 1988).
5. (Cambridge, Mass.: Harvard University Press, 1964).
6. (Cambridge, Mass.: Harvard University Press, l973).
7. (New York: Oxford University Press, 1971).

8. I am not in any sense exempting synthesizers like myself from the assertion that historians have a natural propensity to overgeneralize. Just as the evidentiary or database is typically far narrower than the observations, interpretations, and conclusions that appear in the writings of historians who deal with specialized subjects, so too those historians/synthesizers who generalize about a subject on the basis of the work—appearing in journals and in monographic studies—of other historians draw inferences in their writings that go well beyond what the scholarship/evidence precisely warrants. I am asking both specialists and synthesizers to become more explicit about this discrepancy, to make it clear that *all* historical interpretation involves this kind of overstatement and is thus by nature tentative, suggestive, and incomplete.

CHAPTER 11

1. These assertions are based on scholarship that is focused on Britain and the United States: J. W. Saunders, *The Profession of English Letters* (London: Routledge and Kegan Paul, 1964), Victor Bonham-Carter, *Authors by Profession* (Los Altos, Calif.: William Kaufmann, 1978, 1984, 2 vols.), Nigel Cross, *The Common Writer: Life in Nineteenth Century Grub Street* (New York: Cambridge University Press, 1985), and James L.W. West, *American Authors and the Literary Marketplace Since 1900* (Philadelphia: University of Pennsylvania Press, 1988).

2. For a study of the eclectic character of the writings of professional writers before they became increasingly specialized during the course of the twentieth century, see John Gross, *The Rise and Fall of the Man of Letters: Aspects of English Literary Life Since 1800* (London: Weidenfeld and Nicholson, 1969).

3. It seems to me that three basic types of writing have emerged in the modern world: descriptive, academic, and bureaucratic. Elites that deal with the general public—politicians, journalists, and artists of all kinds—ordinarily use descriptive language. Academics use their conceptual language with each other and their students or with others whom they are trying to influence in their capacity as experts. Bureaucrats of various types have developed a language—used to communicate with each other or with those they serve—that occupies an uneasy position between ordinary or descriptive parlance and academese, with its characteristically elaborate terminologies and conceptualizations. The emergence of bureaucratese is an indication that academic language has had an impact on the wider world, as university- and college-trained graduates apply a learned inclination for creating concepts and terminology to the functioning of large organizations.

Bibliography

Achenbaum, W. Andrew. *Old Age in the New Land: The American Experience Since 1790.* Baltimore, Md.: Johns Hopkins University Press, 1978.

Ahlstrom, Sidney. *A Religious History of the American People.* New Haven, Conn.: Yale University Press, 1972.

Anderson, Benedict. *Imagined Communities: Reflections on the Origins and Spread of Nationalism.* London: Verso, 1983.

Arensberg, Conrad. "American Communities." *American Anthropologist* 57 (1955): 1143–1162.

Arensberg, Conrad. "The Community as Object and as Sample." *American Anthropologist* 63, no. 2 (1961): 241–264.

Argersinger, Peter H. "The People's Past: Teaching American Rural History." *History Teacher* 10 (May 1977): 403–424.

Baltzell, E. Digby. *Philadelphia Gentlemen: The Making of a National Upper Class.* Glencoe, Ill.: Free Press, 1958.

Baltzell, E. Digby. *Puritan Boston and Quaker Philadelphia: Two Protestant Elites and the Spirit of Class Authority and Leadership.* Cambridge, Mass.: Harvard University Press, 1987.

Bender, Thomas. "Wholes and Parts: The Need for Synthesis in American History." *Journal of American History* 73, no. 1 (June 1986): 120–136.

Blewett, Mary H. *Men, Women, and Work: Class, Gender, and Protest in the New England Shoe Industry, 1780–1910.* Urbana, Ill.: University of Illinois Press, 1988.

Blumin, Stuart M. *The Emergence of the Middle Class: Social Experience in the American City, 1760–1900.* Cambridge, England: Cambridge University Press, 1989.

Bodnar, John. *The Transplanted: A History of Immigrants in Urban America.* Bloomington: Indiana University Press, 1985.

Bonham-Carter, Victor. *Authors by Profession.* Los Altos, Calif.: William Kaufmann, 1978.

Boorstin, Daniel J. *The Americans: The National Experience.* New York: Random House, 1965.

Boorstin, Daniel J. *The Americans: The Democratic Experience.* New York: Random House, 1973.

Braudel, Fernand. *On History.* Chicago: University of Chicago Press, 1980.

Braudel, Fernand. *Civilization and Capitalism: 15th–18th Centuries.* New York: Harper and Row, 1981–1984, 3 vols.

Braudel, Fernand. *The Identity of France:* Volume One—*History and Environment.* New York: Harper and Row, 1988.

Brown, Delmar. *Nationalism in Japan: An Introductory Historical Analysis.* New York: Russell and Russell, reprint, 1977 (1955).

Bruchey, Stuart. *The Wealth of a Nation: An Economic History of the United States.* New York: Harper and Row, 1989.

Butler, Jon. *Awash in a Sea of Faith: Christianizing the American People.* Cambridge, Mass.: Harvard University Press, 1990.

Chatterli, Krishnalal. *The National Movement in Modern China.* Calcutta: F.K.L. Mukhopadhyay, 1958.

Chavan, R. S. *Nationalism in Asia.* New Delhi: Sterling Publishers, 1973.

Colley, Linda. *Britons: Forging the Nation, 1707–1837.* New Haven, Conn.: Yale University Press, 1992.

Commager, Henry Steele. *The Empire of Reason: How Europe Imagined and America Realized the Enlightenment.* New York: Oxford University Press, 1977.

Commercial Atlas and Marketing Guide. Chicago: Rand McNally, any year.

Cross, Nigel. *The Common Writer: Life in Nineteenth Century Grub Street.* New York: Cambridge University Press, 1985.

Curti, Merle. *The Growth of American Thought.* New York: Harper and Row, 1943.

Curti, Merle. *The Roots of American Loyalty.* New York: Columbia University Press, 1946.

Dalzell, Robert F. *Enterprising Elite: The Boston Associates and the World They Made.* Cambridge, Mass.: Harvard University Press, 1987.

Davis, David Brion. *The Problem of Slavery in Western Culture.* Ithaca, N.Y.: Cornell University Press, 1966.

Davis, David Brion. *The Problem of Slavery in the Age of Revolution, 1770–1823.* Ithaca, N.Y.: Cornell University Press, 1975.

Dawley, Alan. *Class and Community: The Industrial Revolution in Lynn.* Cambridge, Mass.: Harvard University Press, 1976.

Degler, Carl. *At Odds: Women and the Family in America from the Revolution to the Present.* New York: Oxford University Press, 1980.

Diamond, William. "On the Dangers of an Urban Interpretation of History." In Eric Goldman, ed., *Historiography and Urbanization.* Baltimore, Md.: Johns Hopkins University Press, 1941.

Dublin, Thomas. *Women at Work: The Transformation of Work and Community in Lynn, Massachusetts, 1826–1860.* New York: Columbia University Press, 1979.

Elkins, Stanley. *Slavery: A Problem in American Intellectual and Institutional Life.* Chicago: University of Chicago Press, 1959.

Evans, Richard J. *The Feminists: Women's Emancipation Movements in Europe, America, and Australasia.* London: Croom Helm and New York: Barnes and Noble, 1977.

Faler, Paul. *Mechanics and Manufacturers in the Early Industrial Revolution: Lynn, Massachusetts, 1780–1860.* Albany, N.Y.: State University of New York Press, 1981.

Fischer, David Hackett. *Growing Old in America.* New York: Oxford University Press, 1977.

Fischer, David Hackett. *Albion's Seed: Four British Folkways in America.* New York: Oxford University Press, 1989.

Fite, Gilbert. "Expanded Frontiers in Agricultural History." *Agricultural History* 35 (October 1961): 175–181.

Fogel, Robert. *Without Consent or Contract: The Rise and Fall of American Slavery.* New York: W. W. Norton, 1989.

Frederickson, George. *White Supremacy: A Comparative Study in American and South African Slavery.* New York: Oxford University Press, 1981.

Friedland, William H. "The End of Rural Society and the Future of Rural Sociology." *Rural Sociology* 47, no. 4 (1982): 589–608.

Galpin, Charles. "The Development of the Science and Philosophy of American Rural Society." *Agricultural History* 12 (July 1938): 195–208.

Gans, Herbert J. "Urbanism and Suburbanism as Ways of Life: A Re-evaluation of Definitions." In Arnold Rose, ed., *Human Behaviour and Social Processes.* Boston: Houghton Mifflin, 1962.

Greenfeld, Liah. *Nationalism: Five Roads to Modernity.* Cambridge, Mass.: Harvard University Press, 1992.

Greven, Philip. *Four Generations: Population, Land, and Family in Colonial Andover, Massachusetts.* Ithaca, N.Y.: Cornell University Press, 1970.

Gross, John. *The Rise and Fall of the Man of Letters: Aspects of English Literary Life Since 1800.* London: Weidenfeld and Nicholson, 1969.

Gross, Neal. "Sociological Variation in Contemporary Rural Life." *Rural Sociology* 13 (1948): 256–269.

Guttman, Allen. *From Ritual to Record: The Nature of Modern Sports.* New York: Columbia University Press, 1978.

Guttman, Allen. *A Whole New Ball Game: An Interpretation of American Sports.* Chapel Hill: University of North Carolina Press, 1980.

Haber, Carole. *Beyond Sixty Five: The Dilemma of Old Age in America's Past.* Cambridge, England: Cambridge University Press, 1983.

Handlin, Oscar. *Facing Life: Youth and the Family in American History.* Boston: Little, Brown, 1971.

Harris, Neil. *The Artist in American Society: The Formative Years, 1790–1860.* Chicago: University of Chicago Press, 1966.

Hillery, George A., Jr. "Definitions of Community: Areas of Agreement." *Rural Sociology* 20 (1955): 111–1213.

Hobsbawm, Eric. *Nations and Nationalism Since 1780: Programme, Myth, Reality.* Cambridge, England: Cambridge University Press, 1990.

Hofstadter, Richard. *The Progressive Historians: Turner, Beard, and Parrington.* New York: Knopf, 1968.

Hollinger, David. "American Intellectual History: Issues for the 1980's," In Stanley I. Kutler and Stanley N. Katz, eds., *The Promise of American History: Progress and Prospects.* Baltimore, Md.: Johns Hopkins University Press, 1982.

Kaufman, Harold F. "Toward an Interactional Conception of Community." *Social Forces* 38 (1959): 8–17.

Kett, Joseph. *Rites of Passage: Adolescence in America, 1790 to the Present.* New York: Basic Books, 1977.

Kevles, Daniel J. *The Physicists: The History of a Scientific Community in Modern America.* New York: Knopf, 1987.

Knights, Peter. *The Plain People of Boston, 1830–1860: A Study in City Growth.* New York: Oxford University Press, 1971.

Kohn, Hans. *American Nationalism: An Interpretive Essay.* New York: Macmillan, 1957.

Kolb, John H. *Emerging Rural Communities: Group Relations in Rural Society/A Review of the Wisconsin Research in Action.* Madison: University of Wisconsin Press, 1959.

Kolchin, Peter. *Unfree Labor: American Slavery and Russian Serfdom.* Cambridge, Mass.: Harvard University Press, 1987.

Lampard, Eric. "American Historians and the Study of Urbanization." *American Historical Review* 65 (October 1961): 49–61.

Lerner, Gerda. *The Majority Finds Its Past: Placing Women in History.* New York: Oxford University Press, 1979.

Levine, Daniel. *Poverty and Society: The Growth of the American Welfare State in International Comparison.* New Brunswick, N.J.: Rutgers University Press, 1988.

Levine, Lawrence W. *Highbrow/Lowbrow: The Emergence of a Cultural Hierarchy in America.* Cambridge, Mass.: Harvard University Press, 1988.

Lingeman, Richard. *Small Town America: A Narrative History.* New York: G. P. Putnam's Sons, 1980.

Lipset, Seymour Martin. *The First New Nation: The United States in Historical and Comparative Perspective.* New York: Basic Books, 1963.

Lipset, Seymour Martin. *Continental Divide: The Institutions and Values of the United States and Canada.* New York: Routledge, 1990.

Lockridge, Kenneth. *A New England Town/The First Hundred Years: Dedham, Massachusetts, 1636–1736.* New York: W. W. Norton, 1970.

Lubove, Roy. "The Urbanization Process: An Approach to Historical Research" *Journal of the American Institute of Planners* 33 (January 1967): 33–39.

Lynch, Kevin. *The Image of the City.* Cambridge, Mass.: MIT Press, 1960.

Marsden, George. *Religion and American Culture.* New York: Harcourt Brace Jovanovich, 1990.

May, Henry F. *The Enlightenment in America.* New York: Oxford University Press, 1976.

McDean, Harry C. "Professionalism in the Rural Social Sciences, 1896–1919." *Agricultural History* 58, no. 3 (1984): 373–392.

McNeill, William H. *Polyethnicity and National Unity in World History.* Toronto: University of Toronto Press, 1986.

Meinig, D. W. *The Shaping of America: A Geographical Perspective of 500 Years of History, Vol. 1: Atlantic America, 1492–1800.* New Haven, Conn.: Yale University Press, 1986.

Miller, Michael K., and Luloff, Albert E. "Who Is Rural? A Topological Approach to the Examination of Rurality." *Rural Sociology* 46, no. 4 (1981): 608–625.

Monkkonen, Eric. *America Becomes Urban: The Development of U.S. Cities and Towns, 1780–1980.* Berkeley: University of California Press, 1988.

Nagel, Paul. *One Nation Indivisible: The Place of the Union in American Thought.* New York: Oxford University Press, 1966.

Nagel, Paul. *This Sacred Trust: American Nationality, 1798–1898.* New York: Oxford University Press, 1971.

Nash, Gary. *Red, White, and Black: The Peoples of Early America.* Englewood Cliffs, N.J.: Prentice-Hall, 1974.

Novak, Barbara. *Nature and Culture: American Landscape and Painting, 1825–1875.* New York: Oxford University Press, 1980.

Nye, Russell B. "Changes in Twentieth Century Rural Society" *Midcontinent American Studies Journal* 10, no. 1 (1969): 25–40.

Olson, Philip. "Rural American Community Studies: The Survival of Political Ideology" *Human Organization* 64, no. 4 (1964): 342–350.

Perry, Lewis. *Intellectual Life in America: A History.* Chicago: University of Chicago Press, 1984.

Pessen, Edward. *Riches, Class, and Power Before the Civil War.* Lexington, Mass.: D. C. Heath, 1973.

Picou, J. Steven, et al. "Paradigms, Theories, and Methods in Contemporary Rural Sociology." *Rural Sociology* 43, no. 4 (1978): 559–583.

Pinkett, Harold T. "Government Research Concerning Problems of American Rural Society" *Agricultural History* 58, no. 3 (1984): 365-372.

Potter, David M. "The Historian's Use of Nationalism and Vice-Versa" *American Historian Review* 67 (1962): 924–950.

Redfield, Robert. *The Little Community.* Chicago: University of Chicago Press, 1956.

Reiss, Albert J., Jr. "The Sociological Study of Communities." *Rural Sociology* 24 (1959): 118–130.

Rendall, Jane. *The Origins of Modern Feminism: Women in Britain, France, and the United States, 1780–1860.* London: Macmillan Education, 1985.

Rosenberg, Charles E. *The Care of Strangers: The Rise of America's Hospital System.* New York: Basic Books, 1987.

Ross, Dorothy. *The Origins of American Social Science.* Cambridge, England: Cambridge University Press, 1991.

Russo, David J. *Families and Communities: A New View of American History.* Nashville, Tenn.: American Association for State and Local History, 1974.

Russo, David J. *Keepers of Our Past: Local Historical Writing in the United States, 1820's–1930's.* Westport, Conn.: Greenwood Press, 1988.

Rutman, Darret B. "Assessing the Little Communities of Early America." *William and Mary Quarterly* 43, no. 2 (1986): 163–178.

Ryan, Mary P. *Womanhood in America: From Colonial Times to the Present.* New York: New Viewpoints, 1975.

Saunders, J. W. *The Profession of English Letters.* London: Routledge and Kegan Paul, 1964.

Schlesinger, Arthur M., Sr. "The City in American Civilization." In *Paths to the Present.* New York: Macmillan, 1949.

Schnore, Leo F. "The City as a Social Organism." *Urban Affairs Quarterly* 1, no. 03 (March 1966): 58–69.

Schroeder, Fred E.H. "Types of American Small Towns and How to Read Them" *Southern Quarterly* 19, no. 1 (1980): 104–135.

Shafer, Boyd. *Nationalism: Myth and Reality.* New York: Harcourt, Brace, and World, 1955.

Shafer, Boyd. *Faces of Nationalism.* New York: Harcourt, Brace, and World, 1972.

Shafer, Byron E., ed. *Is America Different?: A New Look at American Exceptionalism.* Oxford: Clarendon Press, 1991.

Simpson, Richard L. "Sociology of the Community: Current Status and Prospects." *Rural Sociology* 30 (1965): 127–149.

Smith, Anthony D. *The Ethnic Origins of Nations*. London: Basil Blackwell, 1986.

Smith, Page. *As a City upon a Hill: The Town in American History*. New York: Knopf, 1966.

Smith, Page. *Daughters of the Promised Land: Women in American History*. Boston: Little, Brown, 1970.

Starr, Paul. *The Social Transformation of American Medicine*. New York: Basic Books, 1982.

Stilgoe, John. *Common Landscape of America, 1580 to 1845*. New Haven, Conn.: Yale University Press, 1982.

Summers, Gene F., Seiler, Lawrence H., and Clark, John P. "The Renewal of Community." *Rural Sociology* 35 (June 1970): 218–231.

Sutton, Willis A., and Kolaja, Jiri. "The Concept of Community." *Rural Sociology* 25 (1960): 197–203.

Swierenga, Robert. "The New Rural History: Defining the Parameters." *Great Plains Quarterly* 1, no. 4 (1981): 211–223.

Swierenga, Robert. "Theoretical Prospectives on the New Rural History: From Environmentalism to Modernization." *Agricultural History* 56, no. 3 (1982): 495–502.

Tannenbaum, Frank. *Slave and Citizen: The Negro in the Americas*. New York: Knopf, 1947.

Thernstrom, Stephen. *Poverty and Progress: Social Mobilization in a Nineteenth Century City*. Cambridge, Mass.: Harvard University Press, 1964.

Thernstrom, Stephen. *The Other Bostonians: Poverty and Progress in the American Metropolis, 1880–1970*. Cambridge, Mass.: Harvard University Press, 1973.

Trachtenberg, Alan. *The Incorporation of America: Culture and Society in the Gilded Age*, New York: Hill and Wang, 1982.

Tyrrell, Ian. "American Exceptionalism in an Age of International History." *American Historical Review* 96, no. 4 (October 1991): 1031–1055.

Wallerstein, Immanuel. *The Modern World-System*. New York: Academic Press, 1974–1988, 3 vols.

Warner, W. Keith. "Rural Society in a Post-Industrial Age." *Rural Sociology* 39, no. 3 (1974): 306–318.

Warren, Roland L. *The Community in America*. Chicago: Rand McNally, 1963.

Weber, Adna. *The Growth of the City in the Nineteenth Century: Study in Statistics*. New York: Macmillan, 1899.

West, James L.W. *American Authors and the Literary Marketplace Since 1900*. Philadelphia: University of Pennsylvania Press, 1988.

Wiebe, Robert. *The Segmented Society*. New York: Oxford University Press, 1975.

Wilentz, Sean. *Chants Democratic: New York City and the Rise of the American Working Class, 1788–1850*. New York: Oxford University Press, 1984.

Wilkinson, Rupert. *The Pursuit of American Character*. New York: Harper and Row, 1988.

Wirth, Louis. "Urbanism as a Way of Life." *American Journal of Sociology* 44 (July 1938): 1–24.

Woodward, C. Vann, ed. *The Comparative Approach to American History*. New York: Basic Books, 1968.

Zelinsky, Wilbur. *Nation into State: The Shifting Symbolic Foundations of American Nationalism.* Chapel Hill: University of North Carolina Press, 1988.

Name Index

Subject Index

industrialization 23, 24, 111
industry 38, 43, 69, 111
inequality 14, 23, 34, 98, 101
injustice 101
instability 103
institutional communities 87
intellectual 2, 3, 8, 11, 22, 38, 41-44, 46,
        48-50, 54, 61, 74, 76-78, 87,
        91, 95, 96, 98-101, 103, 107,
        123, 126, 128
interdisciplinary 42

Japan 30
jazz 8, 38, 46
journalism 77, 107, 120
journalists 9, 48, 79, 97, 114, 122
justice 78, 101

knowledge 17, 77, 78, 105, 111, 121,
        123, 125, 126

labor 17, 43, 44, 54, 69, 70, 75, 94, 98,
        104
language 7, 9, 17, 19, 24, 29, 32, 34, 41,
        47, 50, 92, 95, 100, 103, 105,
        112, 115, 120-122, 125, 126
Latin America 30, 37
legitimacy 13, 21, 22, 102
leisure 24, 38, 45, 74, 78, 97, 103, 104
liberalism 19, 34
liberty 3, 18, 19, 23, 33, 34, 100, 101
life cycle 106
life passages 75
linguistic 8, 30, 31, 47, 93
literature 58, 121
local community 17, 55, 58, 68, 69, 72,
        76, 78-81, 83, 84
local government 43, 62, 63
localism 80
love 54, 55, 57, 78, 104, 127

majorities 102
males 15, 18, 106
material culture 66, 105
media 77

medicine 38, 42, 43, 45, 48, 92, 105
middle class 10, 11, 23, 24, 45, 72
Midwest 68
military bases 64
minorities 18, 19, 35, 102
Mississippi River Valley 85
mobility 34, 35, 71, 84, 103, 113

nationalism 7, 8, 29-36, 38, 41, 44, 47, 48,
        50, 54, 80, 92
nationalists 8, 30, 46
nations 3, 7-10, 12, 13, 18, 22, 27, 29-38,
        41-50, 53, 54, 57, 59, 62, 64, 67,
        79, 80, 92-97, 110
native Americans 8, 46
nature 104
neighborhoods 34, 57, 60, 70-72, 74, 76, 79,
        84, 92
New England 17, 18, 37, 44, 55, 68, 75, 76,
        111
normality 102, 127
North America 10, 33-35, 37, 44, 46, 48, 56,
        64, 70-72, 82-84, 119
novelists 8, 114, 121, 123
novels 121

occupations 2, 7, 17, 19, 23, 27, 32, 47, 50,
        56, 65, 66, 84, 87, 92-94, 97, 112,
        120, 121
old [the] 15

Pacific Coast 68, 83
persistence 44, 98, 103, 121
philosophy 8, 9, 29, 38, 43, 46, 58, 100, 103,
        126
physical 57, 65, 66, 68, 69, 71, 74-79, 104,
        110, 121, 123
place communities 81, 83-88
planned communities 69
Platonic 110
playwrights 8, 79, 121, 123
political 2, 3, 7-16, 21-23, 25, 29-39, 41-49,
        53, 54, 57-59, 61-65, 67-72, 75-78,
        80, 86-88, 91-101, 103, 104, 107,
        124
political communities 3, 45, 64, 71, 86

About the Author

DAVID J. RUSSO is a Professor of U.S. History at McMaster University in Hamilton, Ontario, Canada. He is the author of *Families and Communities: A New View of American History* (1974) and *Keepers of Our Past: Local Historical Writing in the United States* (Greenwood Press, 1988).

ISBN 0-313-29682-0

90000>

EAN

9 780313 296826

HARDCOVER BAR CODE